Praise for 30 D

To say that Deuteronomy is my go to book for devotional reading would not be accurate. Yet after reading Dr. Rogers book *30 Days to Deuteronomy*, that has all changed. The way that Dr. Rogers approaches Deuteronomy is not only insightful but extremely practical and applicable for living the Christian life. As a minister that has the privilege of proclaiming God's Word, the illustrations alone are worth the investment in this book. When I have the opportunity to share with the pastors of my state, I will be sure to have them read this scholarly and inspiring work. I have the deepest appreciation for Dr. Rogers and his book, *30 Days to Deuteronomy*.

—Timothy C. Patterson
Executive Director
Baptist State Convention of Michigan

Many believe Deuteronomy is the most influential book in the Old Testament, so the book is a key to unlocking all of the message of the first half of the Bible. Deuteronomy reflects the heart of the Bible--God's covenantal love for his people and his people's love for God expressed in faith and obedience that brings blessing and reward from God. This relationship with God is what makes life worth living. Dr. Matt Rogers has provided clear and careful explanations of the message of Deuteronomy in these devotional studies and thoughtful reflection on how the book is to be applied to our daily lives.

—Dr. Gary E. Yates
Professor of Biblical Studies/Old Testament,
Director of Th.M Program
Liberty University School of Divinity

Before the Israelite people entered into the Promised Land, Moses wanted to remind them of their identity before God and the way of life the LORD was laying out before them through the law. In fact, the very word, Deuteronomy, means "a repeating of the law." Matt Rogers makes this great book of Moses accessible and understandable. He helps us see the great life God has provided for us in relationship to Him. Deuteronomy reveals the great love God has for His people and how we can live a life of love towards Him. Rogers shows us that we can live out that same dynamic relationship with God in our every day lives.

—Dr. Greg Faulls
Senior Pastor, Bellevue Baptist Church, Owensboro, Kentucky

The Book of Deuteronomy is one of the most important books in the entire Old Testament. The sermons and teachings of Moses permeate Israelite teaching, understanding, and religious practice. Time and again the writers of the Old Testament either refer to or allude to the foundational covenant teachings of Deuteronomy. In *30 Days to Deuteronomy*, Matt Rogers has remained true to the teachings of Moses. Rogers honestly reports the harshness of Israel's covenant failures (clearly pointed out by Moses) while at the same time highlighting the deeper message of Deuteronomy (also pointed out by Moses) that while we may fail in our promises, God never does. As is true with all the books in this series, you will be blessed and your faith deepened by reading *30 Days to Deuteronomy*.

—Dr. Chet Roden
Professor of Old Testament, Liberty School of Divinity
Author, *30 Days to Genesis*

30 DAYS TO
DEUTERONOMY

30 Days to Deuteronomy

A Devotional Commentary

Matt Rogers

Seed Publishing Group, LLC
Timmonsville, South Carolina

30 Days to Deuteronomy: A Devotional Commentary

Copyright © 2017 by Matt Rogers

Published by:
Seed Publishing Group
2570 Double C Farm Ln
Timmonsville, SC 29161
seed–publishing–group.com

Edited by:
Bill Curtis, Ph.D.
Dwayne Milioni, Ph.D.

To order additional copies of this resource visit www.seed–publishing–group.com.

Library of Congress Control Number: 2017931516

ISBN–13: 978-0-9968412-8-3

Printed in the United States of America

Dedication

To Corrie, Avery, Hudson, and Willa
Love God's word

Contents

Foreword

I am so glad you picked up this book. Here's why. Octavius Winslow once said, "The religion of the Lord Jesus is valuable only as its power is experienced in the heart." This 30 Day journey through Deuteronomy, one of the Bible's richest and most pivotal books, is designed to help make that happen. And here's more good news: we have a trustworthy guide.

Matt Rogers is more than a friend. He's a guy I admire. He loves his church and the Church. He sacrifices a lot of time encouraging other pastors and people who help start new churches, like me, not to mention the effort he spends creating resources to benefit everyday Christians in their everyday lives. God has not only granted him great insight into the Bible, but a heart that desires to see people experience God's best. He will help you understand this ancient text penned hundreds of years before the arrival of Jesus by explaining the historical context and theological themes, as well as expose its relevance for our relationships, workplaces, neighborhoods, and of course, our relationship with God.

God designed his Book to be a mirror revealing the very core of our lives (James 1:22-25). This journey will encourage you to look within. It assumes we don't have it all together. It assumes we need grace and reveals how Deuteronomy consistently points us to the King of grace, Jesus Christ. There are many well-timed, piercing questions that will lead you to pause and ask: Where should I be encouraged by God's grace in my life? In what ways should I seek more of God's grace in my life? You will be challenged to pray and live differently.

Foreword

I am confident you will be rewarded for the short time you invest each day to go deeper with God through his Word. That's why I look forward to reading this book with my wife, my kids, and the people I mentor as they walk with Jesus. To enjoy the journey is to enjoy the very reason we were created: for more and more and more and more of God himself. Enjoy the journey as you enjoy him.

—Dr. Tanner Turley
Lead Pastor, Redemption Hill Church (Medford, MA)

Preface

As a teenager, I was familiar with the stories of the Bible, or so I thought. I heard the Bible read and preached many times, though I'd not spent any time reading it myself. Following my conversion, though, I had a seemingly insatiable hunger to understand God's word. I picked up the Bible and did what you do with all books—I started at the beginning and tried to read straight through. I was driven, but even then I didn't make it out of the book of Numbers. The Bible was overwhelming, intimidating, and confusing.

But, I did not stop. I skipped forward to the New Testament and began reading Matthew's Gospel. As I read, I noticed all these little notes throughout my Bible. Before each sentence, and sometimes in the middle of sentences, there were little letters and numbers that pointed me down to the bottom of the page. There, I found all kinds of references to other passages of Scripture. In Matthew 4 I read about Jesus' temptation by the devil in the wilderness. In this passage, Matthew placed several of Jesus' statements in quotations marks, and, upon further reading I observed that Jesus was quoting the book of Deuteronomy. For the first time I remember thinking, "This whole book is connected."

And I was right. As I continued to read, I learned that the Bible was one big, united story. The different authors, writing to unique audiences at specific times in history, were telling the unified story of God's work to save fallen humanity. Even more than that—the Scriptures found in the Old Testament actually helped to understand

Preface

God's character, man's sin, and the salvation made possible by Jesus Christ.

I was hooked. Since that time, the Bible has been an ever-increasing treasure for me. Every time I read God's word I see his brilliance on display. Therefore, I'm grieved when people assume that the Bible is too difficult for them to understand or when they neglect God's word and leave it to collect dust on the coffee table. I'm committed to work to help people read and understand God's word for themselves and, for that reason, I decided to write *30 Days to Deuteronomy.*

I love the book of Deuteronomy because it provides one the most vivid pictures of the grace of God found in the Bible. The themes of the book illuminate the work of Jesus like none other. In it, you will see your sin and God's love in fresh and new ways.

I'm also excited about this 30 Days series. Books like *30 Days to Acts, 30 Days to James,* and others are meant to provide readers with a succinct and clear, daily devotions through the books of the Bible. Our hope is that they will aid you in your reading and encourage you to persevere in your time in God's word.

Finally, I'm thankful for the work of Seed Publishing Group, a publisher committed to bringing great resources to both individual Christians and the local church (seed-publishing-group.com). As part of that commitment, they are partners with The Pillar Network for church planting (thepillarnetwork.com). One dollar from each sale of *30 Days in Deuteronomy* goes directly to church plants throughout North America.

May God use this book to capture your heart with the beauty of his word and may you treasure it all the days of your life.

—Matt Rogers

Time to Move

Deuteronomy 1:1–8

*The LORD our God said to us in Horeb, "You have
stayed long enough at this mountain."*
Deuteronomy 1:6

Life moves. Of course, there may be sporadic moments when it feels like time stands still, but the reality
is that life is always moving. People are moving, cars are
moving, jobs are moving, communication is moving, and
on and on the list could go. The pace of life in the modern
world is dizzying. This movement may mask the fact that
many people don't have the slightest idea where they are
going. Like a toy ship tossed into a raging river, many of
us get swept away in the current of life without stopping to
consider the direction in which our lives are moving.

The Bible is a book about movement. Primarily, it
is a book about the movement of God to pursue sinful humans and save them by the power of his love. God's saving
work then propels his people into a life of transformation
and mission. Like every living being, God's people grow
and change. God's people move.

The book of Deuteronomy is a book about the movement of God's people, the nation of Israel. The book opens
with the vast nation poised on the brink of the land God
promised to the descendants of Abraham long ago (Gen
17:8). At one time, it seemed that they would never realize this promise. Not long before, the nation was enslaved

1

> *The book of Deuteronomy is a book about the movement of God's people, the nation of Israel.*

in Egypt and longed for deliverance. God, in a mighty demonstration of his power, overcame the most powerful nation in the known world and led his people to freedom through the Red Sea (Ex 6–14).

From there, they were to quickly move to the Promised Land, where they would dwell in peace and experience the bountiful provision of God. The story told in the Bible, from Exodus 15 to the end of the book of Deuteronomy, describes in horrific detail the failure of the people of God to move as God desired. A journey that should have taken them 11 days took 40 years instead. These intervening years testified to the sinfulness of the people and their repeated inability to walk faithfully with God.

God, on the other hand, kept his promises in spite of the sin of the people. Though an entire generation died in the wilderness as a judgment for their stiff-necked rebellion and unbelief in God's promises, God continued to bring about his good purposes.

Deuteronomy is a collection of sermons to the nation of Israel by Moses—the man who had led them through this convoluted journey. The conclusion of the book of Numbers provides editorial comments on what follows in Deuteronomy, declaring that these are the words of Moses to the people in the plains of Moab just east of the land (Num 36:13).

Now an aged man, Moses stood on the plains of Moab before the children of those who were delivered from slavery in Egypt. His words were poignant and profound, passionate and clear. There, he testified to the awesome faithfulness of God. He reminded them of God's grace in response to their sin and of the glorious privilege of being chosen by him.

The title of this book betrays the beauty of its message. "Deuteros" means "second" and "nomos" means "law." The "second law" was a title derived from Deuteronomy 17:18, where God commanded Israel's future kings to make a copy of the law, so that they would be reminded of his commands to the nation.

While the book recounts the law of God, Deuteronomy is a book about grace. Moses began the book with a reminder of God's kindness to the nation. He had brought them out of slavery, protected them from their enemies, and brought them to Mount Horeb where he gave them his law. After staying at the mountain for two years, God called them to move. God said, "You have stayed long enough at this mountain (v. 6)." The future promise beckoned them to move. The land that was set before them called them forward (v. 7). God's promise to Abraham, Isaac, and Jacob propelled them onward (v. 8).

The book of Deuteronomy, like the rest of the Old Testament, may seem distant and irrelevant to modern readers. The names and places are unfamiliar, and the implications for believers today may seem unclear. Sadly, this causes many to neglect this beautiful and brilliant testimony to God's grace. Jesus and the authors of the New Testament demonstrated the significance of this book, since they quoted from it more than any other book in the Bible. Why did the authors of the Bible care so much about the earlier Scriptures? Why should we?

Anchored in the opening verses of this book is one answer to this question. The God who leads the people is the God of history. He is the Creator God, who made Adam and Eve and established them as his image-bearing representatives (Gen 1:26–28). He is the covenant-making God, who called Abraham to himself as an act of grace and promised his unending love to him and his descendants (Gen 12:1–3). He is the God who, against all odds, provided children for barren parents (Gen 21:22) and protected them from destruction (Gen 22). He is

> *While the book recounts the law of God, Deuteronomy is a book about grace.*

> We should develop great confidence in God's ongoing care and leading in our lives when we read about God's sovereign care of his people at this critical juncture in history.

the God who took Joseph from an Egyptian prison to second-in-command of the most powerful nation in the world, thus preserving his people (Gen 50:20). He is the God who delivered a vast nation from slavery and led them to freedom and covenant with him (Ex 6:7).

Not only is he the God of the past, he is also the God of the future. Paul said that all of those who know Christ through faith and repentance are children of Abraham and recipients of the promises God made to this man of faith (Gal 3:29). The years of history between God's promise to Abraham and his present work to save the lost testify to his faithfulness to save sinners and bless them with innumerable evidences of his grace. We should develop great confidence in God's ongoing care and leading in our lives when we read about God's sovereign care of his people at this critical juncture in history.

Not only has the nature and character of God remained unchanged, but also the propensity of humans for sin has remained unchanged as well. Because of Adam's sin, all people are born dead in sin, rightfully deserving of God's wrath (Eph 2:1–3). As a result, all people sin for similar reasons and in similar ways. The wayward, stiff-necked foolishness of the nation of Israel holds up a mirror for our lives, revealing the factors that lead us towards rebellion.

God's faithfulness and human sin are the main factors that drive the movement of people through life. At times, our sin obscures our view of God's faithfulness. We may lose heart, believing that our faith struggles and failures have irrevocably tarnished God's good purposes for us. During the days ahead, I hope that God will use your study of Deuteronomy to do exactly what it was intended to do for its original audience: remind you of the unchanging faithfulness of a God of overwhelming grace.

Food for Thought Your life is moving, and you can't stop it. This thought will either paralyze you with apprehension or motivate you to change and grow. Where is your life going right now? Are you pleased with where you are headed? Do you believe that the current direction of your life is aligned with God's good purposes and plans for you? As you consider the journey of the nation of Israel throughout the book of Deuteronomy, you may need to reflect on this question repeatedly and ask the Spirit of God to bring about much needed changes in your life.

The movement of the people of God, in the Old Testament and today, demands a series of choices. All people are faced with the same **Faith in Action** choices: to respond to God's grace through faithful obedience or to disobey and turn away from him. You've taken a good step by beginning a serious study through the book of Deuteronomy. Ask someone you know and love to hold you accountable for the next 30 Days as you read this book. Ask them to text or email you every day to remind you to spend this time with the Lord. Remember, accountability is a good thing—it helps us replace bad habits with good ones.

Prayer

Spend time asking God to birth a desire in your heart to see and respond to his grace. Ask him to open your eyes so that you can see his stunning faithfulness in the pages of Scripture and in the story of your life. As he does, ask that you would respond to him in awe-struck worship.

A Faithful God and a Fallen People

Deuteronomy 1:26–33

*Yet in spite of this word you did
not believe the LORD your God
Deuteronomy 1:32*

It would be nice if people always kept their word. Every day people make all sorts of promises to one another—some large and some small. We promise to be home at a certain time, to get the kids from soccer practice, or to grab some milk from the store. We also live based on larger promises. Some have promised to be faithful to their spouse, others have promised to pursue excellence in their college studies, and still others have promised to faithfully fulfill their obligations as an employee. These promises are meant to guide our actions, inform our emotions, and chart the course for our lives.

Yet, we know that we fail to live up to our promises. Sometimes this failure does not have a great effect. If we forget milk from the store, our spouse might be frustrated, but our failure to keep this promise might simply cost us another trip to the store or a breakfast of dry cereal. It's no big deal, right?

On the other hand, our inability to keep our promises may have life-altering implications in different areas.

> " The good news of the Bible is that the basis of our hope is not found in our promises but in God's promises. "

Breaking the covenant promise of marriage through adultery has implications for everyone involved— likely for the rest of their lives. Someone's sloppy, inattentive work ethic may cost them their job, and, because of that unfaithfulness, thrust their family into economic turmoil and pain. Simply put: failure to keep certain promises can change your life forever.

Unfortunately, many people understand Christianity in this way. They may wrongly believe that at the foundation of the Christian faith is a two-way promise between God and those who claim to follow him. They promise to be faithful to God and keep his laws, and, in turn, he promises to reward them with his love, care, protection, and blessing.

If this were the message of the Bible, it would not be good news; rather, it would be terrifying news. Imagine how often you fail to keep your promises to God. Just reflect back on the last week. Have your thoughts, emotions, and actions perfectly reflected God's character? Few of us will stand up to that test. We know that we have failed and continue to fail.

The good news of the Bible is that the basis of our hope is not found in our promises but in God's promises. This was Moses' point at the outset of the book of Deuteronomy. He spends the first three chapters reminding the people of the continued failure of the nation to keep their promises to God.

This has to be painful for the nation. Now, gathered on the plains of Moab across the Jordan from the Promised Land, they were forced to hear these stories of failure again. Much like a child who has been caught in sin, they likely rolled their eyes as Moses recounted the shameful and foolish history of the nation.

Those gathered around Moses were not the original per-petrators of most of this sin. Their parents, the first gen-eration brought out from slavery in Egypt, were the ones about whom Moses spoke. That generation had been on the brink of the Promised Land before (v. 19–20). God brought them through the wilderness and commanded them to go in and take possession of the land (v. 21). That was over three decades ago. What happened?

Moses tells us what happened. The people failed to take the land because they did not trust that God would keep his promises. Instead, they sent spies into the land to assess whether or not they could go in and possess it (v. 22–24). Military strategy of the day would base its tactics on the reports of advance teams of spies. Here, it seems that the report of the spies was a foreshadowing of the dis-trust that would cripple the nation.

The spies came back with a good report—the land was a good land just as God said. "Yet you would not go up (v. 26)." Those words testify to the unbelief of Israel. They knew that the land was good, and they knew that God had promised it to them. Yet, they would not go up. They heard of the giants in the land, and their hearts melted in fear. Unbeknownst to them, God was overwhelming the hearts of the pagan nations with fear; fear of his might and pow-er displayed through Israel (Josh 2:11). Conversely, God's people cowered in fear because of their sin. As a result, they refused to trust in God's promises.

Moses reminded the people that they had every rea-son to trust God. He was the one who would fight on their behalf (v. 30). He was the one who would care for them as a father does his child (v. 31). He was the one who demonstrated his presence to them and showed them the path to follow (v. 32). Still, they did not believe.

> *Rather than trusting God, walking in obedience, and experiencing his blessings, the nation would now die in the wilderness.*

> He is the always faithful, never-changing rock on which we can build our lives and place our faith.

For this reason God judged them. That generation would wander in the wilderness and die there because of their sin of unbelief. Rather than trusting God, walking in obedience, and experiencing his blessings, the nation would now die in the wilderness.

Moses reminded this new generation of their parents' horrific fate to make his same point. His message was simple: "You have been here before, and you'd better not make the same decisions that your parents did. Trust God and obey."

The beauty of these words is that God is the only sure object of our trust. He is the only one who always keeps his promises (Num 23:19). In fact, he can't break his promises. He is the always faithful, never-changing rock on which we can build our lives and place our faith (Ps 89:34).

The faithfulness of God is the basis for the obedience of God's people. Not only that, the faithfulness of God is at the very heart of Christianity itself. Christianity rests on the claim that God will do what he said he would do, even in the face of human sin and rebellion (Rom 5:8). He will not leave his people; he will pursue them in love through the work of Jesus Christ and the power of the Holy Spirit, in order to claim and keep them for himself. And, once saved, they will begin a process of transformation by which God will increasingly remove their sin and conform them to the image of Jesus (Rom 8:28–30). His people can rest assured that he will complete the good work he has begun in their lives (Phil 1:6). All of this happens, not because Christians are perfect and never break their promises, but because of the faithfulness of a God, who always keeps his.

> The faithfulness of God is the basis for the obedience of God's people.

We are prone to making the same foolish choices that Israel made. We know that God is faithful. We have seen his mighty power. We know the joy that he provides. We experience the hope that comes from the knowledge that our sins are forgiven. We look back on our lives and observe the avalanche of Gods grace that has filled our lives.

But in spite of these truths, we often live in doubt, fear, and unbelief. As a result, we disobey God and fail to realize his presence, power, and plans for our lives. Of course, we all know that life can seem overwhelming at times. We live in a world wrecked by Satan, sin, and death. Cancer diagnoses are real. Broken marriages are all too common. Wayward children break our hearts. Sin still clings closely to our formerly depraved hearts. The book of Deuteronomy reminds us that these circumstances do not determine our future or alter the purposes of God. His was, is, and will always be faithful to his promises. Our goal today is to trust that he will do what he always does—keep his word.

Food for Thought Christians are to reflect the character of God. Powered by the Spirit of God, they can do what they otherwise could not do. The faithfulness of God is not meant to make us passive or to cause us to think that our actions do not matter. They do. Our faithfulness to our promises is a direct reflection of our love for God and understanding of his character. In what ways are you failing to keep your promises today? How does the faithfulness of God motivate you to repentance and obedience?

Faith in Action It is impossible to claim the promises of God if we do not know them. What promises has God made to you today? Take a few minutes and see if you can make a list of ten promises that God has made to his children. For example, God promises to never leave or forsake his people (Heb 13:5). And, he promises that no one, not even Satan, will be able to snatch God's children out of his hand (Jn 10:28). List some other promises of God from his Word and reflect on the implications of those great promises for your life today.

Prayer

Thank God that he keeps his promises. Praise him for his faithfulness to you in spite of your sin. Call to mind the great attributes that the Bible uses to describe God and worship him through your prayer today.

The Anger of God

Deuteronomy 1:34–40

*And the LORD heard your words and was angered,
and he swore, "Not one of these men of this evil
generation shall see the good land that I swore
to give to your fathers..."*
Deuteronomy 1:34–35

No one enjoys talking about judgment. It may conjure up images of that time when you were a kid and you lied to your parents, and the consequences have been etched in your memory ever since. Judgment is a word most of us would like to forget.

In the same way, few people like to talk about the judgment of God. Within the church, it has been a topic that most simply ignore. At times it seems like the God we read about in the Bible is angry, malevolent, or just woke up on the wrong side of the bed. We've been taught that God is a God of love, and, as a result, we struggle to understand how God can also act in judgment. Outside of the church, any discussion of the judgment of God is mocked. Moral relativism reigns supreme, so people are left with the notion that if there is a God, he is only a God of grace and love.

The stories of the Bible convey a different description of the character of God. There we meet a God who is both a God of astounding love and of righteous judgment. He does not simply turn a blind eye to sin. Life under God's

> *There we meet a God who is both a God of astounding love and of righteous judgment.*

care is not an extended vacation at your grandparents' house, where you can get away with breaking rules you'd never break at home. Rather, nothing escapes the ever-present eyes of God. He sees and knows all things, even what we would love to hide.

The nation of Israel had some stuff they wanted to hide. Consider the irony of the fact that they were sitting in their tents, murmuring and complaining about the God who had just miraculously delivered them from slavery. The way Moses described the people in the passage is far from flattering—they were unwilling to go up, they rebelled, they grumbled, they were afraid, they did not trust, and they would not listen. Not exactly the way you would expect to see these recipients of God's grace described.

God's response was clear: Moses said that God heard their words and acted. You may find it strange to note that God is "angered" by the actions of the people, but it's important to note that God does not get angry like we do. Our anger is informed by numerous motives. Sometimes we get angry for the right reasons, like when we hear about a heinous crime that has been committed in our community. At other times, we get angry for the wrong reasons, like when someone offends us or our plans don't work out. Even when we get angry for the right reasons, however, we do not always respond in the right way. We are prone to emotional outbursts or shortsighted attempts to get even.

God's anger is different. It is based on his holy character. This means that he always gets angry for the right reasons and always responds in the right ways. The nation of Israel experienced the anger of God firsthand. God judged them for their sin and declared that no one over the age of 20 would be allowed to enter the land he promised their forefathers (v. 35). Yet, God did not revoke his promise of the land altogether. He would keep his promise to the nation despite their sin. Because of their sin, however, all those who acted in unbelief would die in the wilderness. Joshua and Caleb, the two spies who trusted God and told Israel they could take the land, were the only people from that generation who would be allowed to enter. (v. 38–39). As a result of God's judgment, the people were sent back into the wilderness. This "turn" would define the nation—rather than dwelling in a good land and enjoying God's provision, they became wanderers in a harsh land, suffering the just consequences for their sin (v. 40).

Immediately, the people realized their sin and tried to avoid God's punishment. "We messed up," they said. "We'll go take the land now." God was not pleased and warned them against challenging the enemy without his blessing (v. 41-42). They should have known by now that it was God, and not they themselves, who had won all of the victories up to that point (1:30; 3:22; 20:4). Without God's power, Israel was doomed. Their crushing defeat at the hands of the Amorites proved that they were helpless without God. Ironically, he would now go with them into the wilderness. Once again, he would teach them to depend on him and to prepare their children to enter the land.

Our sin is rightfully deserving of God's judgment, too. We are prone to sweep our sin under the rug and pretend that it doesn't exist. Our pride, unbelief, and rebellion, like that of the nation of Israel, necessitate the wrath of a holy God. He cannot turn his back on our sin either.

All people are rightfully deserving of the wrath of God because of their sin (Rom 3:23; 6:23; Eph 2:3). God wants to live in fellowship with us, but his justice requires that he punish our sin. Somehow, God must find a way to both punish sin and redeem sinners. Thankfully, Jesus is God's great answer to the problem

> *God's anger is different. It is based on his holy character.*

> *Our sin is rightfully deserving of God's judgment, too.*

of human sin. Jesus' death on the cross allowed God to "be just and justifier of the one who has faith in Jesus (Rom 3:26)." He is just, because he poured out on Jesus the wrath that was due for our sin. Jesus' heinous death proved that sin does not go unpunished. God is also our justifier. Because his justice was satisfied through the cross, he can now declare those of us who place our faith in Jesus to be both forgiven and justified. We are given the righteous standing of Jesus—God sees us without sin and declares us to be holy. As Paul wrote, "For our sake he made him to be sin who knew no sin, so that in him we might become the righteousness of God (2 Cor 5:21)." Those who have not placed their faith in Christ's work will experience separation from God forever in a place of eternal torment (Mt 25:46). Those who have trusted Christ can know that Jesus has paid the full price for their sin, and as a result, they will not suffer the eternal consequences they deserve.

This does not mean that a believer's sin has no consequences, however. Paul warned the Galatian church, "Do not be deceived: God is not mocked, for whatever one sows, that will he also reap. For the one who sows to his own flesh will from the flesh reap corruption (Gal 6:7–8)." Often, God gives people over to the consequences of their sin and allows them to experience the results of their foolish choices. Sure, a Christian will not be eternally judged for sin, but God can and will discipline them for sin.

For example, a husband who sinfully pursues financial prosperity and accolades in his workplace to the neglect of his family may experience the pain of family dysfunction. A wife who squanders endless hours in gossip may isolate herself from vital relationships and love. A young man who passionately gives himself over to endless hours of pornography may spend the rest of his life battling to discover authentic intimacy in a Christian marriage. A family who rejects a calling to take the gospel of Jesus to an unreached people group may battle depression or discouragement because of their lack of faith. Does this mean that God does not love us? No! In fact, it is a sure sign of his love. He loves with such a ferocious, jealous love that he is intent on destroying anything that may rival our love for him. This should cause us to repent of our sin and plead for God's grace and mercy, rather than trying to fight the battles on our own. When we think of all that God has done for us, it should cause us to worship Jesus—the one who fully satisfied God's justice and made it possible for us to have a forever relationship with him!

> *He loves with such a ferocious, jealous love that he is intent on destroying anything that may rival our love for him.*

Food for Thought Have you repented of your sin and placed your faith in the work of Jesus? Often, people begin studies like this one believing that good works (like reading the Bible) will please God. The problem is that you can never do enough good deeds to earn God's favor. The good news of Jesus is that your sin can be forgiven, not because you are good enough, but because of God's love, grace, and mercy. If you are unsure about the state of your soul before God, please read "Finding L.I.F.E. in Jesus!" at the end of this book.

Faith in Action

You may find yourself experiencing discipline from God because of unconfessed sin in your life. God's discipline is not meant to cause you to work harder in your own strength. If you do that, like the nation of Israel, you will be crushed. God's discipline is meant to drive you to him; you must depend on his strength. Rather than cowering in shame and guilt, confess your sin before God and believe that he loves to lavish his children with grace and mercy.

Prayer Ask God to reveal any discipline that may be in your life today. Spend time in silent reflection, considering the way you are prone to rebel from God and reflecting on the consequences of your actions. If you're experiencing discipline, God's Spirit to grant you genuine repentance, knowing that whatever he is doing is being done for your good. Regardless of whether you're experiencing discipline today or not, commit yourself anew to walk in obedience to God today.

You've Seen This Before

Deuteronomy 2:26–3:11

But the LORD said to me, "Do not fear him, for I have given him and all his people and his land into your hand. And you shall do to him as you did to Sihon the king of the Amorites, who lived at Heshbon."
Deuteronomy 3:2

"Trust me." We use these two simple words all the time, and we use them in a variety of ways:

"There's no need to use the GPS; I know the way to the party. Trust me."

"I'll be at the meeting fifteen minutes early to help you set up. Trust me."

"Yes, I know that I lost my job today and we have no money in the bank, but we will be ok. Trust me."

We've all lived long enough to know that it is risky to place too much stock in these words. Sometimes people are trustworthy; other times we get lost on the way to the party, have no help setting up for the meeting, or don't have enough money to pay the bills.

Trust is only as good as the person making the promise.

The life of a Christian is one of trust in God.

Trust is only as good as the person making the promise.

The words "trust me" could serve as the overall theme of Moses' message throughout the book of Deuteronomy. He is not asking people to trust him. Instead, he is begging the people to trust God. This trust is founded on the character of God and the history of his dealings with the nation of Israel. The end of chapter two and the beginning of chapter three describe two significant episodes in the life of the nation that should have propelled their trust in God to new heights.

Two kings, Sihon and Og, were powerful leaders of nations that Israel had to confront on their way to the Promised Land (Num 21:21–35). First, Moses reminded the nation of their experience with Sihon, king of Hesbon (Deut 2:26–37). Israel asked to pass through his land, but, like Pharaoh in Egypt, Sihon's heart was hardened and he would not show kindness to the people of God (2:30). Not only did Sihon reject the request of the people to pass through the land, but he also led his people into battle against Israel. This king was no match for God. They were soundly defeated—their people killed, their cities destroyed, and their wealth plundered (2:33–35).

Next up was Og, king of Bashan. Like Sihon, King Og led his people into battle against Israel. God told the nation to trust him; he would once again give the king and his land to them (3:2). These enemies of God were destroyed by Israel as a demonstration of his power and might, but this was not an arbitrary act by a vindictive God. The judgment of the nations was rightly due them because of their sin. Like Rahab, they could have trusted in the one true and living God, but they did not (Josh 2:8–14). Therefore, God judged these nations.

These actions were also intended to motivate Israel to trust God. The editorial comments in verse 11 highlight this reality. To make his point, Moses told them that King Og's bed was still in Rabbah. And, guess what? It was a really, really big bed—it was over 13 feet long and 6 feet wide! The contrast is clear. The nation had refused to take the land 40 years earlier, because they were afraid of the giants in the land (1:28). But, Moses reminded the nation that God had killed giants before—even giant kings who slept in giant beds.

Over and over again, God calls each of us to trust him. Trusting God is the basis of our salvation (Is 12:2). We become Christians when we proclaim our trust in God and his plan for our salvation: the person and work of Jesus Christ. From there, the life of a Christian is one of trust in God. The wisdom found in the book of Proverbs begins with the exhortation to "trust in the Lord with all your heart, and do not lean on your own understanding (Prov 3:5)."

This was the very step that the nation of Israel failed to take. They leaned on their own understanding and failed to trust God. They believed that the giants were big and strong; this was true. There were giants in the land, but God was on their side. They had nothing to fear. Dead kings like Sihon and Og should have made this point crystal clear.

The same is true in our lives. We have a long history of God's faithfulness to remember. Everyone reading this book today has been given the gift of life that they neither earned nor deserved. Last night while we slept, God sustained our lives without any help from us. Those of us who know Jesus have a far more miraculous story. God, knowing full well the depth of our sin, brought us from death to life through the finished work of Jesus (Eph 2:8–9). He fought the giants of Satan, sin, and death and emerged victorious. Paul, in the ultimate trash-talking

Like a wasp without a stinger, the ultimate enemies of human existence have been crushed beneath the mighty hand of God.

> *God will use all of the unique circumstances of our lives to conform us to the image of Jesus and to complete the good work that he began in us.*

verse in all of the Bible, taunted these defeated enemies: "O death, where is your victory? O death, where is your sting (1 Cor 15:55)?" Like a wasp without a stinger, the ultimate enemies of human existence have been crushed beneath the mighty hand of God. These realities are true for every Christian.

Furthermore, we can each point to a seemingly endless list of proofs that God has been faithful to us throughout our lives. It could be the way that he has guided us, redeemed our foolish decisions, or brought us through the fires of adversity. One thing is certain—God has been faithful to us in personal ways that demonstrate that he can be trusted. According to Paul, God will use all of the unique circumstances of our lives to conform us to the image of Jesus and to complete the good work that he began in us (Phil 1:6). He will do this, because "God is faithful, by whom you were called into the fellowship of his Son, Jesus Christ our Lord (1 Cor 1:9)." Like Israel's memories of Sihon and Og, you and I can point to foes that have been defeated by our ever-faithful God. As a result, we should trust him without reservation.

But, do we? Unfortunately, we often treat God the same way that we treat our family or friends when they say, "Trust me." Simply put, we doubt if he can be trusted. When we do this, we're prone to rely on our own understanding, and we begin solving problems on our own. This means that we've forgotten the Sihon's and Og's of our own lives; we've forgotten the longstanding history of God's faithfulness; we've forgotten that Satan, sin, and death are defeated; we've forgotten that God has never let us down.

> *The Bible is not a collection of stories about some ancient deity; it's the united story of the only true God whose faithfulness never changes.*

God uses the history of Israel to remind us of his trustworthiness. The Bible is not a collection of stories about some ancient deity; it's the united story of the only true God whose faithfulness never changes. For Moses' listeners, these stories were meant to motivate them to take the land. Today, these stories are meant to empower us to trust in God's faithfulness and walk by faith with him.

Food for Thought Many people believe that trust must be earned before it is given. Our sinful nature assumes that people will let us down, so they must earn our trust over time. God should be trusted for no other reason than the simple fact that he is God. But, he has also earned the trust of his people. History stands as a testimony to the fact that God can be trusted. Every time we read our Bibles, we meet this faithful God. In light of the history of God's faithfulness from cover to cover in the Bible, what is stopping you from trusting him today?

Faith in Action It can be helpful to spend time gathering stories about God's faithfulness. For the people in Deuteronomy, the stories of Sihon and Og were certainly important. These were powerful kings who were defeated by God. For us, these stories may fall flat. We don't know Sihon and Og, and we won't be called upon to overthrow the nations and take a strip of land that God had promised us. We all have stories about God's faithfulness, however. Spend some time making a list of the ways that God has proven he can be trusted in your life. Be specific, and share this list with someone this week.

Prayer

As you reflect on your list, ask God to remind you of his faithfulness each day this week. Seek to allow these stories of God's faithfulness to cultivate trust in your heart. Repent of the ways you have trusted in your own understanding this week, and ask God to teach you that his wisdom is far greater than anything you can devise on your own.

Sin's Influence

Deuteronomy 3:23–29

*Go up to the top of Pisgah and lift up your eyes
westward and northward and southward and
eastward, and look at it with your eyes, for you
shall not go over this Jordan.*
Deuteronomy 3:27

Moses is one of the greatest leaders in the Bible.
Few would have believed this was possible given the events
surrounding his birth. His mother placed her infant, He-
brew son into a basket and sent him down the river in order to protect him from Pharaoh's death squads (Ex 1:16).
Miraculously and ironically, he was discovered and res-
cued by Pharaoh's daughter and raised in Pharaoh's pal-
ace. Ultimately, he would lead God's people out of slavery
in Egypt and toward the realization of God's great promise
to Abraham (Ex 2:1–10). In fact, Moses himself doubted
his ability to lead God's people. Even when God assured
him of success, he was hesitant to trust God (Ex 3:1–12).
Yet, God used him to accomplish great feats and lead the
people to the brink of the Promised Land.

Moses was not perfect, however. His lack of trust
in God was clearly seen in Numbers 20 when he confronted the nonstop grumbling of the people he was called to
lead (Num 20:2–3). They had no water, and once again
they claimed that they would have preferred death to suffering in the wilderness (Num 20:4). Moses was told to

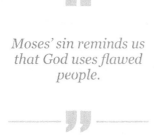

> *Moses' sin reminds us that God uses flawed people.*

call the people together and speak to a rock, and God would provide water to meet their needs. This may sound strange to a modern reader, but Moses had seen God do far greater wonders. He knew that God loved to display his power through miraculous deeds like this (Ex 4:1–9).

In a shocking turn of events, Moses did not obey God. Rather than speaking to the rock, he struck it twice with his staff. God provided water in abundance, but Moses failed. God said, "Because you did not believe in me, to uphold me as holy in the eyes of the people of Israel, therefore you shall not bring this assembly into the land that I have given them (v. 12)." Moses repeated the failure of the people. Like the people he led, he didn't trust God to keep his word. In a seemingly insignificant decision, Moses failed to obey God and took the matter into his own hands. This mirrored the decision that the people made when they came to the Promised Land for the first time. They failed to trust God to give them the land and took matters into their own hands. Interestingly, God disciplined both Moses and the nation of Israel for the same sin.

Moses' sin reminds us that God uses flawed people. The conquest of the Promised Land would not be the result of Moses' flawless leadership, perfect obedience by the people, or a brilliant military strategy. The Promised Land was a gift from God, and God used Moses to accomplish his sovereign plan. The nation could not look to any human leader—not Abraham, Moses, or even David—to provide perfect leadership. Only Jesus, the perfect Son of God, could provide the leadership the people desperately needed.

Moses' sin also demonstrates the responsibility that leaders have to model faith in God before those whom they are called to lead. This includes all leaders, whether pastors, missionaries, deacons, small group leaders, youth leaders, or children's leaders who have a responsibility to model faith in God and obedience to the Scriptures. It includes Christian parents, who are called to lead their children to know, love, and follow God. In Deuteronomy 6, Moses reminded the people of the law God had first given them at Mount Horeb (Ex 20). After reminding them of the pinnacle of the law—the call to love God and love others—Moses reminded the nation that this love should first permeate the families (Deut 6:7–9). Parents were to lead their homes in such a way that their children knew of God's faithfulness, his work in their nation's history, and his grace in giving them his law. Generations would suffer if they failed in this task, because God would visit "the iniquity of the fathers on the children to the third and the fourth generations (Num 14:18; see also Ex 20:5)."

Moses' sin reminds also reminds us that those who know God and have heard his word are responsible to demonstrate and declare the greatness and glory of God. If they do not, both they and those they lead will suffer for their failure.

The reality of principle can be seen in many places. It may be observed in the son of an alcoholic Father, who now struggles with addiction himself. But it can be observed in more subtle ways, too. For instance, parents who consistently neglect the discipline of their children may doom them to a life of foolish behaviors and choices. Similarly, church leaders who apathetically fulfill their obligations on a weekly basis may model lukewarm discipleship that hinders the spiritual formation of their people. James warns that few should become teachers for this very reason—they will be judged harshly for leading others astray (James 1:3).

The sinless One died on behalf of sinful humanity, so that those who place their faith in him and his finished work could live with him forever. Jesus' death and resurrection provide hope for us in spite of our sin.

> *Our ability to lead others is not based upon our own ability to do what is right; rather, it results from an overflow of our deep dependence upon God's grace and mercy.*

These two principles from Moses' life may make you feel hopeless, but you shouldn't. What should you do? You should be reminded of the hope that you have in Jesus. Jesus did what Moses couldn't do. Sadly, the book of Deuteronomy ends with Moses dying outside of the Promised Land (34:1–8). He died as a result of his sin, and in some ways as a representative of the sins of the people.

Like Moses, Jesus died outside of the camp (Heb 13:12). Rejected by many, Jesus died a criminal's death and bore on his body the sins of the people (1 Pet 2:24). He died as a representative for the sin of the people. But, unlike Moses, he had not sinned (1 Pet 2:22). Even when tempted by Satan to doubt God's words, Jesus repeatedly rejected the enemy's ploys and trusted God wholeheartedly (Mt 4:1–11). Each time, Jesus countered Satan's temptation with a quote from the book of Deuteronomy; he did what Moses and the nation of Israel had been unable to do. The sinless One died on behalf of sinful humanity, so that those who place their faith in him and his finished work could live with him forever.

Jesus' death and resurrection provide hope for us in spite of our sin. We will battle sin as long as we live, but we can live in the reality that Jesus has defeated our sin; God has declared us to be righteous because of Jesus' sacrifice, and we can live for his glory! Our trust in Jesus, then, has a spillover effect into the lives of those whom we love and lead. Our ability to lead others is not based upon our own ability to do what is right; rather, it results from an overflow of our deep dependence upon God's grace and mercy. As we grow in awareness of our sin and of the grace of God through Christ, we will be increasing equipped to influence and lead others. Faithful leaders in the church and in the home are not those who have it all together but those who have learned to depend on Jesus.

Food for Thought *In what ways has the sin of others had an effect on your life? In what ways is your sin having an effect on others? There is no such thing as private sin. While certain sins may be more personal, all sin has an effect on others. Not only does your sin hurt you, lead to God's discipline, and cause you to squander God's blessings, but it can also lead others to follow in your path of disobedience.*

Faith in Action

If you have sinned against someone recently, ask God to help you forgive you as you repent and turn from that sin. If necessary, seek that person out and ask for forgiveness. More than likely, the first place to look is within your own home. Your spouse, children, or extended family are easy targets for your sin, so take time today to repair any relationships that have been damaged by sin.

Prayer

Praise God for Jesus, who did far more than simply set an example of morality for you to follow. He actually lived the life you could not live, in order to make it possible for you to live the life he desires for you. Thank God for sending Jesus for sinners like you (and Moses).

The Gift of the Law

Deuteronomy 4:1–8

And now, O Israel, listen to the statutes and the rules that I am teaching you, and do them, that you may live, and go in and take possession of the land that the LORD, the God of your fathers, is giving you.
Deuteronomy 4:1

Imagine that you are traveling in a foreign country where you don't know the language. Each day is a struggle to do the most basic tasks. You are unsure how to find a restaurant for lunch, hail a taxi to get to your meeting, or pick up a few basic necessities at the store. Everything is unknown and incredibly frustrating. All the worry and stress vanishes, however, if you have someone along who can help. Someone who speaks the language can help you make sense of the otherwise incomprehensible.

The distance between a person and an unknown, foreign language is nothing compared to the distance between sinful people and a holy God. We must know his language in order to understand him, recognize his actions in the world, and discern how we should live. Without his guidance, we're lost.

This is how Moses' audience would have felt. The previous forty years had been tumultuous to say the least.

> *The original recipients of the law would have understood clearly that the law was a gift of grace. It was never designed to be a means of earning God's favor.*

From slaves, to wilderness wanderers, to a walking death camp, they were finally on the edge of the Promised Land. They were now headed into unchartered territory. God told them that the land was a good land, but as far as they knew, it was also filled with giants and massive fortifications. They had no clue what they would find. Once they conquered the land, they would need guidance for how to live as worshipers there.

Moses' instructions, as recorded in Deuteronomy, spelled out the many gifts that God had given the people so that they could enjoy the Promised Land rejoice in his presence. Each of these gifts was based upon the glorious truth that the God of Israel is a God who speaks. He had spoken to them in the past, and he would continue to speak to them in the present (5:2–3). The God of Israel stood in stark contrast to the idols of the nations, who "have mouths, but do not speak (Ps 135:15)." This God reveals both his word and his ways to his people.

Earlier, Moses told the people that God gave them his word so that they might both live and take possession of the Promised Land (4:1). These "statutes and rules" were given as a gift of God's grace (4:1). For most of us, the words "statutes" and "rules" do not have a positive connotation. We often view them as restrictive and arbitrary, and in turn, are prone to view God as a cosmic killjoy. But, like an interpreter in a foreign land, God's rules provide guidance for how to live safely in a chaotic world.

> *Obedience was a response to the favor they had already been shown.*

God's self-declaration, which preceded Moses' restatement of the 10 Commandments, reminded the people of his powerful work in their history and their lives (5:6). He was the one who brought them out of slavery and fulfilled his promises to Abraham, Isaac, and Jacob. Moses reminded them of the foundational commands that would shape the obedience of the nation.

Centuries later, a lawyer asked Jesus for the most important commandment. Jesus replied, "You shall love the Lord your God with all your heart and with all your soul and with all your mind. This is the great and first commandment. And a second is like it: You shall love your neighbor as yourself. On these two commandments depend all the law and the Prophets (Mt 22:36–40)." Many have pointed out that the 10 Commandments follow this basic structure: the first four commands focus on loving God, and the remaining six focus on loving people.

The original recipients of the law would have understood clearly that the law was a gift of grace. It was never designed to be a means of earning God's favor. Instead, obedience was a response to the favor they had already been shown. For former slaves, these laws would have been filled with hope. They had once lived in a culture that worshiped an abundance of gods, but now they would be free to focus their worship on the one true God (5:7). In Egypt, the God of Israel was devalued and mocked, but now the nation could manifest God's name rightly (5:11). Slaves had no rest; they were forced to work to fulfill their masters' every whim. Now, however, they would be given the gift of Sabbath rest (5:12). Slavery tore families apart, devalued human life, and exploited the people economically. Now, finally, they could love their families, protect all life, and create a culture that valued all people (5:16–21).

The people knew that God's greatness was put on display by these laws. They were stunned that the God of history would speak to them and still allow them to live (5:25–26). And, they knew that

> *We worship a God who speaks.*

Jesus is God the Word made flesh. He came to dwell among a sinful people and to show the world what God is like.

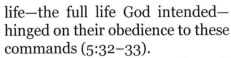

life—the full life God intended—hinged on their obedience to these commands (5:32–33).

While much separates the culture of Deuteronomy from that of our day, one thing remains true—we worship a God who speaks. The Scripture reveals that God has graciously spoken in two additional ways. First, God has spoken through Jesus. The author of Hebrews wrote:

> Long ago, at many times and in many ways, God spoke to our fathers by the prophets, but in these last days he has spoken to us by his Son, whom he appointed the heir of all things, through whom also he created the world. He is the radiance of the glory of God and the exact imprint of his nature, and he upholds the universe by the word of his power. After making purification for sins, he sat down at the right hand of the Majesty on high (Heb 1:1–3).

Jesus is God the Word made flesh. He came to dwell among a sinful people and to show the world what God is like (Jn 1:1–14).

Second, God has spoken through the Bible (Ps 19; 119). God, in his kindness, saw fit not only to speak to people long ago, but also to preserve his words for us throughout all generations. Not only that, he has preserved it in languages that we can understand. The Bible testifies to the redemptive plan of God through his Son, Jesus, who died and was raised again to rid the world of Satan, sin, and death. The Bible is a powerful tool that God uses to teach, reprove, correct, train, and prepare his people for good works (2 Tim 3:16–17). The Bible is a gift of God's grace to his church today.

Yet, we neglect this gift all too often. Around the world, there are millions of people who have still never heard of the Bible, much less had the opportunity to read it in their own languages. Meanwhile, many of us have ten copies lying around our houses. Sadly, spiritual disciplines like Bible reading often become drudgery to us. We know that we should do it, but if we're honest, we really don't want to. Why is this?

Perhaps this feeling of drudgery results from losing the awe that the God who created us would also speak to us. We take it for granted. We assume that we've heard it before, or that we have more important stuff to do. We forget the gift and leave it unopened. Thankfully, your journey through the book of Deuteronomy demonstrates that God has birthed a passion in you to open the gift of the Bible. You may be awakening to the beauty of the word and the wisdom of God contained in its pages. Or, you may already be growing weary, ready to put it back on the shelf. Don't lose heart. Remember that God's word is a gift of grace to an ever-wayward people like you and me. Treasure the gift and continue to train your heart to worship a God who is so kind that he would speak to you.

Remember that God's word is a gift of grace to an ever-wayward people like you and me.

Food for Thought Plans matter. No one drifts toward discipline. If you want to grow in your love for God's word, you must spend time each day reading and meditating on the Scriptures. Do you have a plan? If not, pick a specific time each day when you will commit at least fifteen minutes to reading a passage of Scripture and asking God to speak to you through his word.

Faith in Action

We have a unique opportunity through our relationships to expose others to the gift of the God's word. As you read this week, seek out someone you know, a coworker or neighbor, and share a verse of Scripture with him or her. Speak about the way that God has encouraged or challenged you with his word, and trust that God's Spirit will continue to give you a chance to share in the days ahead.

Prayer

Thank God for his kind gift of the Bible. Praise him that he gave you a book that you could both read and understand. Ask him to convict you of times when you waste this gift through sloppy living or passivity.

Watch Yourself

Deuteronomy 4:15–24

*Take care, lest you forget the covenant of the LORD your God,
which he made with you, and make a carved image, the form
of anything that the LORD your God has forbidden you. For
the LORD your God is a consuming fire, a jealous God.*
Deuteronomy 4:23–24

There are few sights more beautiful in the world
than a pristine waterfall. The sheer size, speed, and vol-
ume of water create a majestic backdrop for any tourist.
If you hike to the top of the waterfall, you are likely to see
signs posted at the edge of the river that tell you to watch
your step. The continual flow of water over the rocks lining
these rivers makes them extremely slick—so slick that one
missed step could cost you your life.

Three times Moses repeated a similar warning to
the nation of Israel. He began in verse 15 by commanding
them to "watch yourselves very carefully." In verse 19 he
said, "Beware," and finally in verse 23 he challenged them
to "take care." These warnings sound strange on the brink
of a land that was "a good and broad land, a land flowing
with milk and honey (Ex 3:8)." On the surface it wouldn't
seem that they had anything to fear, except getting fat on
the bountiful provision of the land. Yet, God knew that
there was an enemy lurking in the land far more perni-
cious than the danger of gorging on honey.

> *Since the creation of the world, God's people had been prone to worship as God objects that were not God.*

The inhabitants of the land worshiped false gods, and God knew that his people had always been drawn to idols. The history of the nation was littered with rebellion and judgment due to their insatiable appetite for them. While God gave Moses his law at Mount Horeb, the people of God resorted to this diabolical practice because they were afraid that God had abandoned them (Ex 32). Aaron, of all people, led the nation to build their own god and worship it as the one who had delivered them from Egypt.

The roots of their idolatry go back much further than the debacle at the wilderness mountain, however. Since the creation of the world, God's people had been prone to worship as God objects that were not God. In fact, Paul traced the root of all human sin to idolatry. He wrote that all people "exchanged the truth about God for a lie and worshiped and served the creature rather than the Creator, who is blessed forever (Rom 1:25)!" Even today, people make this fatal exchange anytime they take God's good gifts and twist and distort them into objects of worship.

There is no end to the types of objects that people can worship in God's place. In the Old Testament, the nations worshiped man-made idols made to look like created beings. Moses' list included idols made in the likeness of humans, animals, birds, creeping animals, fish, the sun, the moon, and the stars (Deut 4:16–19). This list included all of the beings God made in his original creation—this time in reverse order (Gen. 1). The point is clear: Anything made by God can become an object of idolatry.

Notice, nothing in this list is bad in and of itself. These things were created by God and called

> *Anything made by God can become an object of idolatry.*

good (Gen 1:31). But people excel at taking good things and worshiping them. For example, parents may be tempted to take the God-given gift of a child and turn him or her into an idol. These little angels can quickly become the axis around which life revolves, and before you know it, the parents shape their every decision and action solely on the basis of its impact on their kids. In so doing, God can quickly take a back seat to the family.

God gives good gifts to his children (Jam 1:17), but these gifts are meant to prompt people to worship the gift-giver and not the gifts themselves.

Work may also become a source of idolatry. Rather than working as an act of worship to God, we can worship work itself. Men and women may spend countless hours in the office, incessantly check their email and banging away at the computer keyboards—all in an effort to climb the corporate ladder. The list of common idols could go on and on, including education, college football, politics, sex, or any of a laundry list of good things made by God.

Moses pointed out the folly of idolatry—these things aren't God, and they aren't to be worshiped. In fact, they will collapse under the weight of human worship. God gives good gifts to his children (Jam 1:17), but these gifts are meant to prompt people to worship the gift-giver and not the gifts themselves.

It's interesting to note that the people were drawn to worship the idols that were revered among the nations. God knew that the obsessions and possessions worshiped in the surrounding culture could quickly captivate the hearts of his people. The same is true for you and me. Not only does our sin nature lead us to worship idols, but the prevailing culture of our day has a gravitational pull on our hearts as well. If you're like me,

When we worship, we ascribe worth to someone or something.

> *From the moment our feet hit the floor in the morning until the time we close our eyes at night, our hearts will be worshiping something—either the true and living God or something else.*

the siren call of technology cries out to my heart and lures me away from God on a daily basis. Without constant vigilance and care, I ignore the warning signs and give myself to the worship of idols.

How do you know when idols have a grip on your heart? Consider the nature of worship itself. The word is derived from the Old English word weorthscipe. Our English word "worth" is at core of its meaning. When we worship, we ascribe worth to someone or something. We ascribe worth to objects every day: our spouses, children, jobs, money, possessions, and pleasure. Sadly, these things may also become objects of worship. Remember, worship isn't some mystical practice; it's very concrete. In reality, we can't stop worshiping. From the moment our feet hit the floor in the morning until the time we close our eyes at night, our hearts will be worshiping something—either the true and living God or something else.

The consequences for idolatry are stark. God promised to treat Israel the very way that he would treat the idolatrous nations (Deut 4:26–27). If Israel gave themselves to their idols, God would kick them out of the land that he had given them as a gift. You would think that the 40 years Israel spent in the wilderness would be enough to teach them the value of the land. But, idolatry was so attractive to them that it would not be long before those warnings became a reality (Jer 44).

There is only one truth great enough to propel you away from a life of idolatry (Deut 4:32–40). Moses reminded the people that their God was the one true God. He is the only being who is worthy of the affection of all people. God's desire is that his people "may know that the Lord is God; there is no other beside him (4:35)."

It sounds counterintuitive, but the best way to fight idolatry is to fall in love with God. As your heart grows warm with passion for God, you will see that other objects of worship pale in comparison. Your sinful longing for these idols will not dissipate completely as long as you live in this world, but you will learn that they promise far more than they can deliver and always leave you wanting more. Only God can fully satisfy the desires of the heart (Ps 107:9).

Food for Thought What is your go-to idol? What is your heart drawn to worship? Idols are personal and unique to each of us. Still, they are hard to see. We are often blinded by our idols and captivated by worshiping them. To make matters worse, we are prone to rationalize our idols existence by convincing ourselves that we can worship both them and God at the same time.

Faith in Action

Some of God's greatest gifts are the good friends who can point out your idols. They can help you peer into the corners of your lives that you're prone to overlook or excuse. Reach out to your spouse or a good friend and ask him or her to point out any areas in your life where they believe that you are susceptible to idolatry. Be careful to listen, and avoid excuses. Allow God's Spirit to bring conviction and change.

Prayer

Ask God to help you see your idols before it's too late. Pray that He would reveal the ways that you tolerate and worship idols. Confess these idols before God in prayer, and ask him to help you see how much greater he is than any idol.

Obedience
is Worship

Deuteronomy 5:22–33

You shall be careful therefore to do as the LORD your God has commanded you. You shall not turn aside to the right hand or to the left.
Deuteronomy 5:32

The warnings of Moses continue. He had just warned Israel to be careful that they not fall prey to idolatry. Next, he warned them that they must be careful to walk faithfully with God. This shouldn't surprise you. Even someone with a casual understanding of Christianity would say that it's important for Christians to obey God. What they are likely to miss, however, is the motive for that obedience.

Consider the common story of a student who grows up going to a youth group at her local church. She has heard countless sermons, been on many mission trips, and is generally seen as a leader among her peers. But, when she is not with her church friends, she is prone to worldliness and rebellion. She knows that she is living a double life, but the more she does it, the more it feels normal, and she assumes that she is getting away with it. Then, one day her parents catch her in a lie. This discovery exposes another lie, which leads her parents to uncover her secret life.

> Obedience is rooted in God's actions, not man's.

She is stunned, embarrassed, and filled with shame. In response, she makes a commitment to do better moving forward. But her new-found obedience might flow from a variety of motives. She may obey God because she feels guilt and shame for her sin, and she thinks that her "good" actions are a way to appease her nagging conscience. Or, she may obey in order to prove to God, and her friends and family, that she is the good girl they all thought she was before her double life was exposed. In this case, she may obey in order to avoid the consequences that could result from her immorality.

These motives are not altogether bad. After all, we should feel guilt for our sin, desire to honor God with our lives, and fear the consequences of sin. Over time, however, we'll discover that these motives are insufficient for consistent obedience. Over time, the guilt will wear off, the desire to be good will wane, and the consequences will become less disconcerting. We need something more, something greater, in order to sustain our obedience over the long haul.

Moses provided a different motive for the people. He didn't stop pointing out the folly of their sin, their need to please God, or the consequences of their actions, but he did emphasize the chief motive for their obedience: "The Lord our God has shown us his glory and greatness (Deut 5:24)."

Obedience is rooted in God's actions, not man's. God is great and glorious. He has saved and redeemed. He has shown himself to be faithful to his promises time and time again. He is worthy of our obedience.

In fact, obedience is worship. Paul made this point in his letter to the church at Rome. After scaling the heights of the glory of God and his work in salvation, he turns his focus to the way these realities shape the lives of

God's people. There he wrote, "I appeal to you therefore, brothers, by the mercies of God, to present your bodies as a living sacrifice, holy and acceptable to God, which is your spiritual worship (Rom 12:1)." Then, Paul listed the many forms of obedience that should be evident in one's Christian life: serving the church, loving the saints, rejoicing in suffering, giving to meet the needs of the suffering, honoring governmental leaders, avoiding idolatry, and following the example of Christ (Rom 12–15).

The word "therefore" alerts us that all of these actions are based upon the truth of God's grace established Romans 1-11. He emphasized this point with the phrase "by the mercies of God," which demonstrated obedience is always empowered by God's mercy.

The description "living sacrifice" served as an umbrella term to describe the various areas of obedience Paul commanded. The idea of a living sacrifice is a bit of an oxymoron. How can someone be a living dead thing? Well, this is the very quality that Jesus said would mark all of his people. Luke's gospel records these words from Jesus: And he said to all, "If anyone would come after me, let him deny himself and take up his cross daily and follow me. For whoever would save his life will lose it, but whoever loses his life for my sake will save it (Luke 9:23–24)."

A Christian must learn to deny himself or herself. Jesus' imagery would have been shocking to his first century listeners. Jesus asked them to take up their own cross, a brutal instrument of death, and be willing to put themselves on it. This process, according to Jesus, was the path to life.

The idea of a living sacrifice also demonstrated that obedience to God is holistic. It's not as if part of yourself can be sacrificed while other parts are not. Your entire life, body and soul, is to be a living sacrifice to the One who sacrificed all for you.

Obedience is worship.

Finally, this action is "holy and acceptable" to God. It's an act

Your entire life, body and soul, is to be a living sacrifice to the One who sacrificed all for you.

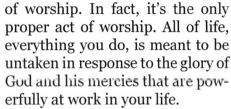

of worship. In fact, it's the only proper act of worship. All of life, everything you do, is meant to be untaken in response to the glory of God and his mercies that are powerfully at work in your life.

So, what does this have to do with our teenager who was just busted in her sin? Everything. Her only hope for sustained obedience is a great awareness of the glory of God. Let's assume for a minute that she's a Christian. If so, she is the unworthy recipient of the mercies of God through Christ. She has been brought from death to life, and her eternal destiny is secure. Every day she lives, she is indwelt by God's Spirit and given the hope, joy, peace, and love that flow freely to all those who are united with Christ. These realities must grip her heart in order for her to fight sin and pursue holiness on a daily basis. The beauty of the good news of Jesus must capture her affections. She must "behold the glory of the Lord" so that she will be "transformed into [Jesus'] image from one degree of glory to another (2 Cor 3:18)."

It may be, however, that her sin reveals that she's not a Christian after all. She may have placed her hope in her ability to be a good person. If so, then continuing down the path of morality will only entrench this false message. God may use a person's sin as an opportunity to expose the fact that they've never received the mercies of God. Clearly, no one can live out of the mercies of God if they have not first received the mercies of God. If she's lost, then the right first step for our fictitious teenager is to bow in repentance and admit her sin before God. She should own up to her inability to live a perfect life and profess her faith in the work of Jesus to pay the price that her sin deserves (1 Jn 1:9). In this way, she would become a child of God and the unworthy recipient of the glorious mercies of God (John 1:12).

The nation of Israel had been promised a deliverer, who would one day fulfill God's promise to rid the world of Satan, sin, and death forever. They longed for that day; they didn't know it would be fulfilled in the future through the person and work of Jesus Christ. Yet, their obedience was still rooted in the mercies of God. They, too, were the unworthy recipients of the mercies of God, having been delivered from Egypt and given a new land. In the mean time, they were called to obey every one of the Lord's commands as they looked forward to the day when God's plan would be made clear. On the other side of the cross and the empty tomb, we have far greater evidence of God's mercies than they. As a result, we who know Jesus should offer our lives as a living sacrifice, because that is the only reasonable response to such astounding mercy.

> *All of life, everything you do, is meant to be untaken in response to the glory of God and his mercies that are powerfully at work in your life.*

Food for Thought What do you do when you sin? How do you respond? Reflect back over the last week and notice the trends in your life. Perhaps you will notice that you respond with guilt, shame, or condemnation, or that you redouble your efforts to try to be good again. What would change if your first response to sin were to think on the mercies of God?

Faith in Action Some who are reading this devotional will approach their Bible reading and the Christian faith in general as another box on their morality checklist. Perhaps you started this book after a season of rebellion and apathy and are plodding through Deuteronomy in hopes that you will figure out how to get your life together. Your sin and morality may reveal a far deeper issue. It may demonstrate that you do not know Jesus in the first place. If so, talk to God in prayer about the state of your soul before him and assess whether or not you have received the mercies of God. Then, read "Finding L.I.F.E. in Jesus" in the appendix of this book.

Prayer

Praise God for his mercies to you through Christ. Reflect on the magnitude of grace and mercy you have received through the work of Christ. Confess your cavalier attitude toward the mercy of God, and ask God to captivate your heart with his love.

Tell the Story

Deuteronomy 6:4–9

*You shall teach them diligently to your children, and shall talk
of them when you sit in your house, and when you walk by
the way, and when you lie down, and when you rise.*
Deuteronomy 6:7

We've probably all played the telephone game as
kids. A leader whispers a secret message in the ear of one
of the kids at the front of the room. Then, one by one, the
message makes its way around the room as one kid whispers the message to another. After the message has made
its way around the room, the last kid repeats the message
to the entire group in hopes that it matches what was said
at the outset of the game. In most cases, a message like
"Every Easter I eat too many candy-corns", becomes "A
very evil toy eats men and unicorns." The point of the game
is to demonstrate the way that messages get jumbled and
distorted as they are passed from one person to another.
The telephone game exposes a truth about humanity—we
struggle to clearly transmit messages to other people, even
really important ones.

The nation of Israel was given some really important messages from God. They received the law (Ex 20) and
were "entrusted with the oracles of God" (Rom 3:2). They
also had a national story of God's redemption. The generation that was brought out of Egypt saw the might and power of God firsthand. Can you imagine the stories you could

The point was clear—talk about God everywhere and all the time.

tell if you had seen the plagues and experienced the Passover? The people were expected to tell the stories of God's faithfulness and communicate the beauty of the law to future generations. In an oral culture, the ability to transmit these stories faithfully would have been of utmost importance. Sadly, this generation passed on a lineage of unbelief and failure.

The home was the first and most important context for transmitting the message. Parents were responsible to teach their children about the character of God the beauty of his law (Deut 6:7). They were to go about this work diligently, knowing that it was critical that their children received the message correctly. This was not a national telephone game—the lives of their children were at stake. They must know about the one true and living God and submit to his law in order to live long in the land God had promised.

The words of Deuteronomy 6:4–9 were known as the Shema and were repeated daily by the Jewish people. This was the first prayer that Israelite children learned because of its clear affirmation of the uniqueness of the one true God and the affect of his covenant upon their daily lives.

For this reason, Moses said that the nation would need to talk abut the Lord when they sat in their houses, when they walked through the city, when they went to sleep, and when they got up in the morning. The point was clear—talk about God everywhere and all the time.

Later, Moses provided fascinating insight on the process for transmitting the message of God. In verse 20, it's the son who came to his parents and asked for an explanation regarding the law. The child didn't ask the parents to tell him the laws, but rather to give him their meanings. The assumption was that the commandments of the Lord would be so pervasive in the home that the child would know what the laws were. As a result, he would want to know why. Why do we behave the way we do? Why is our home centered on the word of God? Why do we talk about the faithfulness of God so often? These would be the natural questions that emerged in a family that was practicing the principles Moses outlined in verse 7. If they were talking about God's character and laws everywhere and all of the time, then it would be natural for the children to want to know why mom and dad made such a big deal about God.

Moses told the people how they should answer these questions. Notice, he didn't tell the parents to give them a list of the laws. He didn't ask them to read the Ten Commandments or memorize the miscellaneous laws found in Deuteronomy 16:18–25:19. Instead, he asked them to tell their son's a story:

> We were Pharaoh's slaves in Egypt. And the LORD brought us out of Egypt with a mighty hand. And the LORD showed signs and wonders, great and grievous, against Egypt and against Pharaoh and all his household, before our eyes. And he brought us out from there, that he might bring us in and give us the land that he swore to give to our fathers. And the LORD commanded us to do all these statutes, to fear the LORD our God, for our good always, that he might preserve us alive, as we are this day. And it will be righteousness for us, if we are careful to do all this commandment before the LORD our God, as he has commanded us (Deut 6:21–25).

They were to remind their children that they were in the land as a gift of God's grace. God had been faithful to them; as a result, they were to be faithful to him. His faithfulness was not some theoretical reality. It was tangible—he made a promise, and he'd been faithful to fulfill his promise. In a very real way, they could say that they were standing on the promises of God when they dwelled in the land.

With every subsequent generation, the telling of that message got harder. No longer could someone say, "I

> *The spiritual climate in your home, the frequency of your family devotions, and the fervency of your family's prayers will reveal your maturity in this area.*

remember walking in the wilderness with mom and dad as a young child. I heard them talking about God's judgment and their hope that I would inherit God's Promised Land." As time passed, their memories of those amazing events waned, and so too did their desire to communicate their meanings to others.

Modern Christians are many, many generations removed from the Exodus story and the original giving of the law. Certainly, we have the testimony of this history and the details of the law in the Bible, but without intentionality, we can find ourselves at the far end of the telephone game. We may find that our clarity on the good news message of the Bible is lacking or that our passion to communicate it has begun to wane. The current status of your home is a helpful diagnostic tool. The spiritual climate in your home, the frequency of your family devotions, and the fervency of your family's prayers will reveal your maturity in this area. Another diagnostic tool would be the questions you get from your children. Do they notice a unique spiritual climate in your home that prompts them to ask questions about why you're different from those who don't know Christ? This is more than simply asking questions about why they have to go to church each week. Rather, do they ask questions about the ways you live your life? Do they ask why church matters to you and why you serve in ministry there? Do they ask why you spend your money serving the poor or helping the weak? Do they ask why you read your Bible and pray with them every day? Do they ask why you don't ever swear like the parents of their friends? Your

> *Your life should be so uniquely informed by the gospel that your children notice and ask questions.*

life should be so uniquely informed by the gospel that your children notice and ask questions.

These conversations in the home should have an effect on the conversations you have outside of the home as well. We should testify to God's faithfulness with non-believing neighbors, coworkers, and friends, while pointing them to the God "who called you out of darkness and into his marvelous light (1 Pet 2:9)." Within the church, we should also speak about the faithfulness of God to our brothers and sisters in Christ. When Paul sent Timothy to lead the church in Ephesus, he emphasized the faithful transmission of the gospel from one generation to the next (2 Tim 2:2). The greatness of God is so vast, and his glory so compelling, that his people should speak about him every chance they get—beginning in their homes and moving outward to the nations.

The greatness of God is so vast, and his glory so compelling, that his people should speak about him every chance they get.

Food for Thought

Imagine that you were playing the telephone game in your home. What might others say they hear when you speak about God? What messages are you sending? Are you teaching your family to understand the word and will of God? Are they hearing the true gospel or some impoverished view of religion?

Faith in Action

Do those around you hear you speak of the Lord? If you don't know, ask them. If you're married, it might be helpful for you to ask your spouse or children to reflect on the spiritual temperature of your home. Ask them how you can grow in saturating your home with the gospel. If you're still single and live with other people, like in a dorm or with a roommate, you can still ask the same question. To what degree is your life reflecting an authentic walk with God, everywhere all the time?

Prayer

Pray that God would protect you from shame and guilt for your shortcomings in this area. We all have a long way to go. Rather than being overwhelmed by your inadequacies, ask God to help you seek out new ways to communicate the gospel to those who matter most in your life.

Never Forget

Deuteronomy 6:10–15

*Then take care lest you forget the LORD, who brought
you out of the land of Egypt, out of the house of slavery.
Deuteronomy 6:12*

There are certain responsibilities that are acceptable to forget—like picking up juice from the store, setting
the timer on the coffee maker for the morning, or returning a phone call to a friend. There are other events that
you'd better not forget—your wedding anniversary, your
kid's birthday, or the deadline for that all-important project. Forgetting any one of these important days is likely to
cost you and cost you dearly.

Moses warned the nation of Israel about forgetfulness once they had conquered the land. This warning
seems almost comical. How could anyone forget the Exodus? Wouldn't the sheer majesty of God's deliverance be
etched forever into the nation's memory? In spite of these
great acts of God, Moses knew that the tendency of the
human heart is to forget God and the great works he has
done.

The warning was contrasted with the promise
of God's bountiful provision in the Promised Land. Moses foreshadowed the day when they would dwell there.
His point was clear—the land was a gift from God (v.10).
The repetition in the verses that follow demonstrate the
overwhelming magnitude of the gift. Notice the number

> The tendency of the human heart is to forget God and the great works he has done.

of times Moses said "did not" in these verses. The nation would get cities they did not build, houses filled with items they did not earn, cisterns they did not dig, and vineyards and olive trees they did not plant (vv. 10–11). You would think that this type of gift would lead former slaves to worship in awe-filled gratitude for the grace of God. Unfortunately, Moses knew that the opposite would happen. Their ample provision would lead them to forget God and the works that he had done for them. They would forget the gift-giver even as they enjoyed the gifts.

You may think this is strange, but consider what happens on Christmas morning in many homes. Parents spend weeks, even months, saving up to buy little Johnny the latest, greatest toy. They wait with expectation as Johnny runs down the steps to see his shiny new gift under the tree. After ripping apart the wrapping paper like a wild animal, Johnny sits enamored with his gift. Johnny runs out into the yard to try it out for the first time as soon as he's ripped it out of the package. Dazed by the bustle of activity, mom and dad sit in the living room staring at one another wondering what just happened. Johnny's passion for the gift caused him to run out of the house without even the slightest "Thank You." He wasn't overjoyed by the love of his parents but by the thrill of the gift.

Obviously, children are drawn to gifts. Perhaps little Johnny would run back some time later to thank his parents. He might even spend the rest of the night hanging out with his dad and playing in the yard with the new toy. Or, he might be too immature to know how to properly communicate his gratitude for such a loving gift.

Johnny's actions expose the tendency of every human heart, however. We may not be drawn to children's toys anymore, but we do long for all sorts of gifts on this earth. Many people long for blessings like good health,

Christians are not promised that tangible blessings on this earth will accompany their salvation.

happy families, or earthly possessions. Spiritually, we may long for joy, peace, hope, and love.

God blesses people with these gifts, because he is the giver of all good gifts (James 1:17). This is not only true for Christians; God's kindness also blesses those who are far from him with an abundance of good things. Life itself is a gift from God. Non-believers may also have their health, families who love them, and material possessions on this earth.

For Christians, the blessings of God flow all the more abundantly. They, too, may have evidence of God's blessing in families, health, or other forms of God's provision. However, God's great gift to Christians is the spiritual blessings that flow from his hand.

First, and foremost, Christians have received the grace-gift of salvation. Paul described this salvation to the church at Ephesus using language similar to that found in Deuteronomy 6. He wrote, "For by grace you have been saved through faith. And this is not your own doing; it is the gift of God, not the result of works, so that no one may boast" (Eph 2:8–9, emphasis mine). Like the conquest of the land, salvation is a gift from God. And, like the nation of Israel, anyone who receives this gift does not earn or deserve it.

The gift of salvation is accompanied by the gift of God's Spirit, who fills every Christian (2 Cor 1:22). The Spirit is at work in believers to produce spiritual fruit in their lives: love, joy, peace, patience, kindness, goodness, faithfulness, gentleness, and self-control (Gal 5:22). These gifts flood the believer's life with the qualities that all people desire. The non-believer may long for peace, but only through a relationship with Christ

Earthly blessings are a poor barometer of the gifts of God.

> *Nothing in this fallen world can separate God's children from the gift of his love. Through Jesus, they can find the gifts of peace, hope, love, and joy.*

can that person know true peace. One trapped in cycles of addiction and brokenness may long for self-control, but that only comes as a gift of God's Spirit.

Christians are not promised that tangible blessings on this earth will accompany their salvation. For some Christians, life may appear harder after they choose to follow Christ. They may suffer persecution for their faith (2 Tim 3:12). They may willingly give up material possessions in order to store up treasure in heaven (Mt 6:20). Like unbelievers, they may battle cancer, face abandonment, lose their jobs, or battle depression, because God doesn't promise to protect Christians from suffering on this earth. Jesus said, "For [God] makes his sun rise on the evil and on the good, and sends rain on the just and on the unjust." (Mt 5:45). Earthly blessings are a poor barometer of the gifts of God.

True, spiritual blessings that are found in relationship with Jesus don't depend on these circumstances. Those who have been saved by God are his, and no one, not even Satan himself, can snatch believers from his hand (Jn 10:28). The indwelling Spirit of God is with Christians, comforting them and pointing them to Jesus at all times (Jn 14:26). Christians can live in hope, knowing that nothing can take these gifts away. Consider Paul's famous words from Romans 8:35–37:

> Who shall separate us from the love of Christ? Shall tribulation, or distress, or persecution, or famine, or nakedness, or danger, or sword? As it is written, 'For your sake we are being killed all the day long; we are regarded as sheep to be slaughtered.' No, in all these things we are more than conquerors through him who loved us.

Nothing in this fallen world can separate God's children from the gift of his love. Through Jesus, they can find the gifts of peace, hope, love, and joy.

Yet, like Johnny, we are all prone to forgetfulness. We quickly run to the blessings of God and forget that they are gifts from his hand. We may fixate on God's physical and spiritual blessings while neglecting him. As we have already seen, these good gifts can become idols that we worship rather than gifts that prompt us to worship God.

Moses' warning to the nation of Israel is true for all people today who experience the blessings of God. We must remain ever vigilant to focus our affections on God and not forget the innumerable blessings that come from his hand.

Food for Thought
What causes forgetfulness in your life? Since we know that our sinfulness will cause us to focus on God's gifts while forgetting him, we must train our hearts to remember him. What good gifts has God given you? What steps could you take today to remember the greatness of the gift-giver?

Faith in Action

Many church hymnals have a song entitled, "Count Your Many Blessings." The idea of the song is quite simple—spend time reflecting on the blessings of God. Make a list in your journal of the gifts that God has given you. Each time you write a new item on the list, remind yourself of the goodness of God in providing you with that blessing.

Prayer

Thank God for being a good gift-giver. Admit your tendency to fall in love with his gifts, and ask him to remind you of all of the stuff you have that you did not earn or deserve. As you think on God's goodness, allow your heart to swell with joy and worship toward him.

Holiness is a Gift

Deuteronomy 7:6–11

For you are a people holy to the LORD your God. The LORD your God has chosen you to be a people for his treasured possession, out of all the peoples who are on the face of the earth.
Deuteronomy 7:6

Every year, thousands of boys and girls fill local orphanages and long for a family to adopt them. Some—the fortunate—find a family where they can be loved and cared for forever. It is a beautiful day to witness the final legal proceedings when the child officially becomes a part of his or her new home. The status of the child changes forever after all of the documents are signed. The verdict pronounced by a judge does far more than change the child's last name—it changes her identity forever.

In the same way, we are told that God chose the nation of Israel. In choosing them, he gives them a new identity that has forever and irrevocably changed the nation. Moses told the nation they are holy. The word "holy" refers to something that is set apart, pure, or distinct. For example, the instruments used for worship in the temple were holy. A table, a pole, or a curtain that was made of common materials was declared "holy" when it was used

Holiness is a God-given identity.

to promote the worship of God's people. These objects were set apart and used only for this purpose.

We do not often use this word when we speak about other people. If we do, it often comes with a negative tone. We might say something like, "She acts like she is so holy, but we all know she's a fake." Or, "He's holier-than-thou." We rarely speak of holiness as a virtue.

I vividly remember the process of joining a new church in my late 20's. I was not on staff at a church for the first time in years, and my wife and I wanted to be a part of a healthy church. After visiting for several weeks, I asked one of the men in the church, whom I respected, to tell me about the lead pastor of this church. He memorably replied, "He's one of the holiest men I've ever met." I'd heard pastors described as effective leaders, passionate preachers, or loving missionaries, but I had never heard someone describe a pastor as holy. Honestly, it felt strange.

Our reluctance to use the word "holy" may stem from the fact that our actions don't seem holy. We know our hearts, and they seem so marred and broken by sin. We know that our actions are often hypocritical, and we sin far more than we'd like to admit.

Clearly, the nation of Israel did not act all that holy either. When God first gave Moses the law, the rest of the nation gathered at the base of the mountain worshiping their jewelry as a god (Ex. 32). From there, their behavior just got worse. The people grumbled and complained all the way to the Promised Land (Ex 16:2; Num 14:2). Rather than taking the land, the first generation acted in unbelief and was sent to wander aimlessly in the wilderness for the next 38 years (Num 14:32–37). This is not exactly the track record you'd expect for a people that God called holy.

This is what God says about his people in spite of their actions, however. They are holy, not based on what they've done or not done, but based upon the fact that they are chosen by God. Long before holiness is something people do, it is something God gives. Holiness is a God-given identity.

God went out of his way to make this point in the verses that follow (Deut 7:7–9). He told the nation that their status had nothing to do with their worth—in fact they were the least of all the peoples of the earth (v. 8). Their identity was based solely on the fact that "the LORD loves you and is keeping the oath he swore to your fathers (v. 8)." They were holy because of the love of God. He conferred identity and status on them in much the same way that an adoptive parent does to a child. Like the land itself, God gave the gift of holiness to his people.

This is not only true of the nation of Israel; it is also true of all of God's people in the church. Paul, in the beginning of his letter to the church at Ephesus, wrote, "He chose us in him before the foundation of the world, that we should be holy and blameless before him (Eph 1:4)." God chose his children and made them holy. This is the divine identity of all of God's people. God does not wait to see whether his people act holy before he sets his affections on them. This is grace.

The introductions to many New Testament letters make his point clearly. Paul wrote, "To the saints who are in Ephesus (Eph 1:1)." He wrote to those in Rome "who are loved by God and called to be saints (Rom 1:7)." In Colossians he wrote, "To the saints and faithful brothers in Christ (Col 1:2)." To the church at Philippi he wrote, "To the saints in Christ Jesus (Phil 1:1)." And, when writing to the sin-infested church at Corinth, Paul wrote, "To those sanctified in Christ Jesus (1 Cor 1:2)."

The word "saint" was Paul's word of choice to refer to God's people in these churches. This word describes "a person acknowledged as holy." Paul called Christians

> *God does not wait to see whether his people act holy before he sets his affections on them. This is grace.*

63

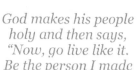

> God makes his people holy and then says, "Now, go live like it. Be the person I made you to be."

saints, even those whose behavior was not saintly. In Corinth, these saints were practicing shameful sexual immorality, destroying unity with factionalism, and getting drunk at the Lord's Supper. Yet, God's grace gave them an identity they did not deserve—they were holy.

The grace-given status of holiness doesn't mean that obedience is unnecessary, however. God still gives his people his Word and expects them to obey. Christians are called to "present your bodies as a living sacrifice, holy and acceptable to God, which is your spiritual worship (Rom 12:1)." As a result, the lives of God's people should be marked by holiness. These holy actions are motivated, empowered, and possible because of a Christian's holy identity. God makes his people holy and then says, "Now, go live like it. Be the person I made you to be."

Returning to the image of adoption may be helpful at this point. Once adopted, the child's legal status changes, and she now belongs to a new family. Her actions did not earn the gift of adoption. But now that she is adopted, her parents would certainly expect her behavior to change over time. Parents would desire for her to obey the house rules, come to the dinner table when the family meal was served, and represent the family well in public. The change of her status ultimately leads to a change in behavior.

The same is true for us as Christians. God makes his people holy. He clothes them in the righteousness Christ earned through his perfect life. Now, God sees his people as holy, blameless, and pure. They are saints. And, as such, they are to live like saints. They are to be what they are.

Why does the distinction made today matter? Isn't the outcome exactly the same—God wants his people to obey him through holy living? Yes. But the motive makes all the difference. If we wrongly assume that we must act holy in order for God to declare us holy, then we have confused the nature of the gospel. And, we will base our thoughts of God on how good (or how bad) we have been. If we've been good, God loves us. If we've been bad, then he doesn't. When the inevitable happens and we sin, then we will hide from God in shame and guilt. When we've been good, we will be prone to self-righteousness and judgment of others whose sin is more prominent than our own. And, worst of all, we will come to view God as the cosmic moral policeman, intent on robbing us of all joy.

But, if we believe that God makes us holy first, then we should be stunned by his grace and love. This awe of God's kindness should cause us to want to obey. Why would we not want to obey someone who loves us that much? And, when we sin (which we will) we know that God still loves us. Our sin—past, present, and future—is forgiven in Christ. We can turn to God, even when we sin, knowing that he has made us holy and nothing can change that.

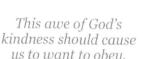

This awe of God's kindness should cause us to want to obey.

Food for Thought What do you do with your sin? What did you do the last time you were aware of your sin? If you find that you wallow in shame, guilt, and despair, then, chances are, you obey for the wrong reasons. If, however, you repent and remind yourself of your standing before God, you will be encouraged by God's grace in your life.

Faith in Action

In order to remind yourself of your God-gven status, read the first two chapters of the book of Ephesians. Write down each word God uses to describe his children. Also, list every word that describes God's actions toward his people. Put this list in a prominent place where you will see it each day in order to remind yourself of how God feels about you.

Prayer

Praise God for his work in your life. If you are a Christian, spend time thanking God for the gift of holiness. Ask him to make you increasingly aware of your holy status and to give you a greater desire to be who you are.

An Enemy Lurking Within

Deuteronomy 8:2–3

*And you shall remember the whole way that the LORD your
God has led you these forty years in the wilderness, that he
might humble you, testing you to know what was in your
heart, whether you would keep his commandments or not.
And he humbled you and let you hunger and fed you with
manna, which you did not know, nor did your fathers know,
that he might make you know that man does not live by bread
alone, but man lives by every word that comes from the
mouth of the LORD.*
Deuteronomy 8:2-3

"You just need to believe in yourself." This statement is an unquestioned maxim of modern culture. Seemingly, low self-esteem is to blame for every problem, including poor test scores, drug addiction, sexual perversion,
and suicide. Many actions once attributed to sin are now
blamed on a person's lack of self-worth.

A razor thin line stands between self-esteem and
pride. You don't have to look far to find pride in our world.
On the football field, athletes will taunt an opponent after making a routine tackle. The public banter between
political candidates or business leaders often amounts to
little more than a forum for prideful posturing. Millions
flex their technological muscles on social media platforms

> *God's holy people are to be humble people.*

every day. The noxious fumes of pride pollute the atmosphere around us every day.

This culture of pride wars against a proper understanding of the gospel. Paul wrote, "For by the grace given to me I say to everyone among you not to think of himself more highly than he ought to think, but to think with sober judgment, each according to the measure of faith that God has assigned (Rom 12:3)." He warned believers against inflated self-esteem. Certainly, all people have worth by virtue of being created in God's image (Gen 1:26–28) and being uniquely knit together by God himself (Ps 139:13–16). Even more, as we saw previously, Christians have worth by virtue of the holy identity given to them by God. But, this God-given worth is not meant to produce sinful pride in God's people. Instead, God's holy people are to be humble people.

According to Moses, this was the point of the wilderness years for the nation of Israel. God did not abandon them in the wilderness; he continued to lead them (8:2). His leadership had a direction and a goal in mind. He wanted to create a humble people (8:2–3). To bring about humility, God allowed them to hunger. Through their hunger, they would know without a doubt that they were entirely dependent on God. After all, it's hard to be proud when you are a rag-tag group of former slaves wandering in a desolate wilderness without any food.

Nonetheless, God consistently fed the people. He let them hunger but never starve. He fed them with food they'd never seen before. Manna came from heaven and in a quantity designed to be sufficient for each day (Ex 16). They were given their daily bread and nothing more. Every morning they were forced to trust God for another measure of gracious provision. In the desert, the basic needs for each day came from God's hand.

Similarly, we can be tempted to forget that all of life is, in fact, a gift from God. We may discover that a trip to the local fast food restaurant exposes our self-sufficiency. We place our order, swipe our card, and a short time later a meal made to our exact specifications appears for us to enjoy. Without thought, we can believe that we earned this food—after all we worked hard and made the money to provide for ourselves! We may forget that our jobs, our paychecks, and the health that allows us to work are all a gift from God. Even a number three combo, large sized with a sweet tea, comes from the hand of God.

Jesus understood this truth. At the outset of his public ministry, Jesus was led into the wilderness where Satan tempted him (Mt 4:1–11). He fasted there for forty days. Satan tempted Jesus three times, but unlike the nation of Israel, Jesus believed God's promises and rejected the enemy's appeals. Each time he was tempted, he responded with a quotation from the book of Deuteronomy (Mt 4:4, 7, 10). He knew he did not have to command the stones to become bread, because God would provide his daily bread (Mt 4:4). He saw no need to put God to the test because he was certain God would always care for him (Mt 4:7). He knew Satan was not worthy of the worship that God alone deserved (Mt 4:10). Jesus succeeded where Israel failed. He modeled a life of humble submission to God. He depended on God to meet his needs.

Before Israel could step into the Promised Land, they had to learn humility the hard way. Forty years in the wilderness were needed. Now, their children sat on the brink of the land. They had the opportunity to relinquish pride and humble themselves before God, in order to enjoy his good provision and live long in the land. And so do we.

Each day, in hundreds of ways, you and I make the choice between pride and humility. We choose to either depend on our-

> *Each day, in hundreds of ways, you and I make the choice between pride and humility.*

> *God's discipline, however, is an act of supreme love.*

selves or trust in God. Often, the most difficult time to make this choice is in seasons of joy rather than in seasons of pain and suffering. When someone is diagnosed with an incurable disease, they are often humbled immediately. Life hangs in the balance as they are forced to depend on others for the most basic tasks. But, give someone a job promotion, some disposable income, a nice house in the suburbs, and a growing retirement plan, and watch what happens. Pride often rears it's ugly head when we least expect it.

God's response to pride is clear. There is nothing more anti-God than a prideful heart, so God must act. He told the nation of Israel that his actions in banishing them to the wilderness, in order to teach them humility, were an act of divine discipline. Discipline, like pride, is probably not your favorite topic. We don't like to think of God disciplining us, and we are tempted to run from his discipline in fear.

God's discipline, however, is an act of supreme love. Moses equated the discipline of God to the love of a father (8:5). Fatherly discipline, when done correctly, is not hate-filled or malicious. Fathers discipline their children because they love them and desire to protect them from pain. Knowing the destruction of sin, fathers correct their children in hopes that they will experience the blessings that come through obedience.

God acts in the same way. He knows that pride is the most sinister enemy to obedience, joy, and blessing. He relentlessly works to expose pride, to crush it, and to produce humility in his people. Because he loves his children, he will consistently bring us to places of weakness, doubt, fail-

> *Because he loves his children, he will consistently bring us to places of weakness, doubt, failure, and need in order to remind us of how little we can do on our own.*

ure, and need in order to remind us of how little we can do on our own.

For this reason, growth in godliness is directly related to growth in humility. At the outset of his ministry, the apostle Paul said, "I am the least of the apostles, unworthy to be called an apostle (1 Cor 15:9)." By the end of his ministry, Paul wrote, "Christ Jesus came into the world to save sinners, of whom I am the foremost (1 Tim 1:15)." Probably the greatest missionary, theologian, and church leader the world has ever seen called himself the greatest sinner—God's grace will do that to a person.

Grace should produce humility in all of us. Self-esteem is not the goal; dependence on God is. God will use whatever means necessary to accomplish this goal in our lives. By his grace, we will be a people who do not think too highly of ourselves because we think too highly of him.

Growth in godliness is directly related to growth in humility.

Food for Thought

Consider the circumstances in your life right now. How is God trying to produce humility in you through your circumstances? What would change about your response if you saw these circumstances as a gift of God to remove pride from your life?

Faith in Action

Pride is blinding. Because of our pride, we struggle to recognize our pride. It takes other people who love us to point out our pride. Have a conversation with someone about pride today. Don't be afraid to do this; you can be assured that they struggle with it, too. Ask them to help you see your pride. As they do, be careful to avoid defensiveness or justification for your actions. Listen, allow them to talk, and ask God's Spirit to help you see and respond well.

Prayer

Confess the sin of pride to God and ask him to produce humility in you. Consider the glorious grace of God revealed in the person and work of Jesus Christ, and allow that to soften your heart. Reflect on the undeserved nature of God's love for you. Worship in prayer before a God who loves a prideful rebel like you enough to work to make you humble.

Downward Growth

Deuteronomy 9:13–21

Furthermore, the LORD said to me, "I have seen this people, and behold, it is a stubborn people."
Deuteronomy 9:13

Every parent knows the scene well. You've just busted your kid breaking the one rule that you've told them twelve hundred times to keep. Before doling out the discipline, however, you sit down and talk to your child. You explain, "Daddy has told you over and over again not to hit your baby sister." The sound of your daughter screaming is all the proof your son needs to know that he is in trouble. Often, your son may dislike the conversation more than the discipline itself. He may roll his eyes, look away, and say with his body language, if not with words, "Dad, could we just get this over with? I don't need you to remind me of that I've done wrong."

It is easy to imagine that Israel may have engaged in a collective eye roll during some of Moses' sermons in Deuteronomy. From the very beginning, he reminded them of the sins of their parents. They were foolish, stiff-necked, and perpetually rebellious. They made the types of mistakes that caused their children to hide their faces in

> *All of God's people need steady reminders of their own sinfulness.*

shame and embarrassment. Their sinful legacy haunted their children to that day.

God cautioned the new generation against forgetfulness when they entered the land (9:6). Their righteousness was not the motive for God's gift of the land. In fact, it was just the opposite. God gave the land to fulfill his promises in spite of the sin of the people. Moses reminded them that they were "a stubborn people" (v. 6) who had "rebelled against the Lord" (v. 7) and "provoked the Lord to wrath" (v. 8).

To make this point, he called to mind two ominous scenes from the history of the nation. First, they failed to trust the Lord and worshiped a golden calf at Mount Horeb (9:13–21). Moses testified to the "hot displeasure" that God had against them and his readiness to destroy his beloved people (9:19).

Second, at Taberah, Massah, and Kibroth-hattaavah the nation continued their waywardness (9:22–24). Their unwillingness to take the land at Kadesh-barnea demonstrated a blatant disregard for God's commands and distrust in his character. According to Moses, the people had "been rebellious against the Lord from the day that [he] knew [them]" (9:24). These are not exactly the glowing commendations you would expect for the holy people of God.

Moses knew that it was vital to remind this younger generation of their parents sinfulness as they entered the land. In pride, they would be tempted to grow apathetic to the commandments of God and forgetful of his promises. They would need constant reminders of their sinfulness to produce the type of humility God desired.

Human nature hasn't changed since Moses wrote Deuteronomy. People in the church commonly assume that truly godly people are those who have their act together—those who don't sin (or at least avoid the "big" sins) and consistently do what is right. Then, when we evaluate our own lives, we know that we don't measure up because we know how sinful we are.

> *Confession of sin forces us to acknowledge how incapable we are of obeying God consistently. It keeps us humble.*

Thankfully, we have been given God's Word to remind us that great men and women throughout history had a deep understanding of their sin. Job said, "I am vile" (Job 40:4). Abraham proclaimed, "I am dust and ashes" (Gen 18:27). Jacob declared, "I am not worthy of the least of all your mercies" (Gen 32:10). Isaiah knew that he was "a man of unclean lips" (Isa 6:5). David, the great King of Israel, called himself a worm (Ps 22:6).

David had ample reason to make this claim. He was a liar, adulterer, and murderer. David was broken before the Lord after God used the prophet Nathan to expose his sin and hypocrisy (2 Sam 12). His prayer, recorded in Psalm 51, beautifully captures the nature of true repentance. He begged God to cleanse him from sin and create in him a clean heart. He acknowledged that his sin was first and foremost against God. He flung himself upon the mercies of God and found the forgiveness he desperately needed. The memory of these sins lingered throughout David's life, producing in him the type of humility that would make David a man after God's own heart (Acts 13:22).

Like Israel and King David, all of God's people need steady reminders of their own sinfulness. When we forgot our capacity to sin, we are prone to self-sufficiency and pride—the mortal enemies of obedience to God. Because of the good news of Jesus, we do not have to wallow in shame, despair, and guilt because of our sin. God doesn't want us to beat ourselves up over our sin. Instead, our propensity to sin should

> *Confession helps us fight sin.*

point our hearts towards the grace God offers. This will keep us humble and dependent on God.

This is why a steady practice of confession is vital for the Christian life. True, our sin—past, present, and future—is forgiven through Jesus. Nonetheless, we need to identify our sin and bring it before God to remind us of the scope of God's grace. Confession of sin forces us to acknowledge how incapable we are of obeying God consistently. It keeps us humble.

Also, confession helps us fight sin. As we bring our sin before God, we are reminded of the common patterns of rebellion in our lives. We see the "sin which clings so closely" and can willingly lay it aside (Heb 12:1). While we will never find perfection this side of eternity, we can mature in Christ-likeness as we fight the sin that God exposes in our lives.

Food for Thought

Why is confession so hard? The simple answer is pride. The very sin that God wants to defeat through confession is often the greatest enemy to confession. When we acknowledge our sins, we take a humble posture before the Lord. Our actions of humility, in time, will foster a humble heart.

Faith in Action

One of the best ways to promote confession in your life is to practice confession to a trusted brother or sister. We are more apt to maintain consistent confession when we force ourselves to speak our sin out loud to someone we trust. Seek out someone in your church family, confess your sin to them, and seek their prayer and accountability today.

Prayer

Confess your sins before God. If you struggle with this practice, find a simple journal and record your sin. As you write, remind yourself of the grace of God that has already forgiven everything you've ever done.

With All Your Heart

Deuteronomy 10:12–22

And now, Israel, what does the LORD your God require of you, but to fear the LORD your God, to walk in all his ways, to love him, to serve the LORD your God with all your heart and with all your soul, and to keep the commandments and statutes of the LORD, which I am commanding you today for your good?
Deuteronomy 10:12–13

As a rule, jobs have clear requirements. New employees receive a list of expectations to fulfill their vocational commitments. This list may include assigned tasks, performance metrics, and training seminars. In return, the employer commits to give the employee a specific compensation package.

Parents often give teenagers requirements as well. These tasks may not be formalized in a written contract like a job, but they are expectations nonetheless. A teenager may be expected to perform tasks around the house, maintain a certain GPA in school, and be home by curfew on the weekends. Those who fail to meet these requirements are disciplined, but those who demonstrate maturity can earn the trust of their parents.

> *God, as the creator and author of all human life, has a plan for his people.*

Even an enjoyable task, like a new hobby, comes with certain requirements. A runner knows that completion of a marathon necessitates certain habits—daily runs and disciplined eating top the list. A writer knows that the art of composing engaging prose requires hours at the keyboard, countless rewrites, and the painstaking process of editing. Requirements are a part of life. Sometimes these requirements come from an external source, like an employer or parent, and sometimes they are produced internally, like the self-discipline of a athlete or author.

Anyone seeking to follow God and to honor him with their life would assume that he, too, would have certain requirements. God, as the creator and author of all human life, has a plan for his people. He has a path for them to walk. He desires his people to live in a certain way.

The Israelites were given clear instructions about these requirements. Throughout the book of Deuteronomy, God gave a wide array of commands to his people. These commands were never intended to be a means by which the people earned God's love. But, because they were loved by God and saved by his grace, God's people would want to obey. They would want to live their lives according to God's plan.

The sheer number of commands found in the Bible may overwhelm some readers. In the book of Deuteronomy alone, one can easily get lost in the requirements. In chapter 10, however, Moses summarized the heart of God's commands. He desired to make God's law crystal clear to the nation of Israel. In chapter 10, Moses provided the people with God's five requirements—fear him, walk in his ways, love him, serve him, and keep his commands.

That's it. Fear, faithfulness, love, service, and obedience are God's requirements for his people. Two of these requirements, fear and love, are characteristics of a per-

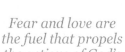

> *Fear and love are the fuel that propels the actions of God's people.*

son's heart. Three of these requirements are actions—faithfulness, service, and obedience. Fear and love are the fuel that propels the actions of God's people. Because we love and fear God, we want to obey.

God knew that his people would need more than moral laws to obey. They would need a new heart. Moses applied the image of circumcision to make this point clearly (10:16). Throughout Israel's history, the practice of circumcision was an external marker for God's people (Gen 17:9–14). In the future, God's people would be set apart in a different way—by a circumcised heart given to them by God. This new heart would do what mere circumcision could never do: it would produce obedience in the heart of God's people. The law would be written on this new heart, and it would be enlivened by God's Spirit (Jer 31:33). God's children receive this new heart through faith and, as a result of this gift, they are now able to obey God has he intended.

Often we are prone to overcomplicate the nature of this obedience, thinking of God as a cosmic taskmaster, intent on making our lives as rigid and dull as possible. Yet, Christian obedience was never intended to be simply an external job description. Certainly, God is external and his requirements are an objective standard for how to live. He made us and knows how our lives are meant to function. However, God's children are driven to obey internally, in much the same way as a runner is motived to train. Their new hearts cause them to desire to obey God and to seek to live the kind of life that honors him.

> *Christian obedience was never intended to be simply an external job description.*

This is the change that all parents hope for in their kids. At first, the requirements in a home should be black and white. The rules are clear and the child is

All obedience to God is rooted in love, and love is only possible through a new heart.

expected to obey—or else. But as the child ages, matures, and experiences the value of their parent's instructions, something may change. The young adult now sees the value of her parent's instructions and seeks to obey out of love for mom and dad. She now knows the wisdom that her parents possess. How much more should God's children know his eternal wisdom and want to obey him?

Jesus knew the necessity of a new heart. In Matthew 22, Jesus was asked a question similar to one found in Deuteronomy 10:12–13. The Pharisees and religious leaders asked Jesus to tell them the greatest commandment in the law. They wanted to know what was most important to God. Jesus answered, "You shall love the Lord your God with all your heart and with all your soul and with all your mind," and "you shall love your neighbor as yourself" (Mt 22:37, 39). Everything else rested on these two commandments. All obedience to God is rooted in love, and love is only possible through a new heart. It was not Jesus' intention to promote external conformity to a list of dos and don'ts. Instead, he pointed them to the same place Moses did—to a new heart given to them by God.

From this new heart, all of God's people will find the power to obey God and keep his commands. We must resist the temptation to assume either that obedience is all that matters or that it doesn't matter at all. While we can't earn God's love through our obedience, because of God's love and the gift of a new heart, we can and should seek to walk in his ways, serve him, and obey him in every aspect of our lives.

Food for Thought *Are you more prone to overemphasize the need for obedience or to underemphasize it? You may consider whether your thoughts are more prone to believe that you can do whatever you want to because God has already forgiven you, or that keeping God's rule is the only way to secure his love. What factors in your life or personality may cause you to accept such a false view of obedience?*

Faith in Action

God's requirements are not complex. Many of us simply fail to respond in obedience to the truths we've learned about God's character. Consider the areas of life that should model a transformed heart— your marriage, speech, purity, or care for others. How should your new heart produce change in these areas? Make a list of a few clear steps you are compelled to make out of love for God.

Prayer

Praise God for the gift of a new heart. Ask his Spirit to bring conviction for areas in your life that do not model that change this new heart should produce. Consider how God's great love for you should produce obedience in your life.

Don't be Deceived

Deuteronomy 11:13–17

*And if you will indeed obey my commandments that I
command you today, to love the LORD your God, and
to serve him with all your heart and with all your soul,
he will give the rain for your land in its season, the
early rain and the later rain, that you may gather in
your grain and your wine and your oil. And he will give
grass in your fields for your livestock, and you shall eat
and be full. Take care lest your heart be deceived, and
you turn aside and serve other gods and worship them;
then the anger of the LORD will be kindled against you,
and he will shut up the heavens, so that there will be no
rain, and the land will yield no fruit, and you will perish
quickly off the good land that the LORD is giving you.*
Deuteronomy 11:13–17

Actions have consequences. Even a small child
knows the truth of this statement. She knows that, if she
screams, mom will give her some milk or a jar of disgust-
ing looking peas. If she continues to scream, her dad will
leave the room or weep in frustration. If she sits on the
dog, man's best friend might become her worst enemy.
Age produces greater consequences to one's choices, but the truth of this maxim remains in place. Actions

> *Actions have consequences.*

continue to have consequences. Now, if the same girl fails to do her homework, then she will fail the test. If she fails to obey her parents, then she will not be allowed to go out on Friday night.

Fast-forward a few years, and the consequences continue to grow in scope. If she marries a godly man who loves her, then she will experience the joy that comes from fidelity. If she marries that rebellious fool that her parents have warned her about, her life will likely be marked by pain and frustration. Working hard in college will produce a degree and a solid job, while failure and passivity will lead to squandered opportunities and wasted gifts.

This "if-then" process is hard-wired into the way God created his world. There is a connection between a person's actions and his or her future. These implications may not be immediately apparent in this life. Sometimes the wicked prosper for a short time (Jer 12:1). The negligent student may land a decent job, and the liar may develop a successful business and have all the best toys money can buy. But, whether in this life or in eternity, a person's actions will have consequences (Heb 9:27).

On the other hand, Jesus' sacrifice dealt with the curse and consequences of sin for the people who believe in him. The wrath of God they deserved was placed on Christ (Rom 5:9; 1 Th 5:9), and they will never have to experience it. This does not mean that there are no consequences for the sin of God's people. Moses warned the nation of Israel in the book of Deuteronomy that their sin would have lasting effects on their future in the land of promise. Should they rebel against God, they would be kicked off the land in the same way that God expelled the nations before them (Deut 4:25–26). Years later, the Assyrians crushed the northern tribes of Israel, and then in 586 BC, the Babylonians destroyed the southern tribes of Judah. The people of God chose to live in blatant rebellion, and as promised, God doled out the consequences. God was unwilling to allow his people to profane his name through ongoing and willful disobedience, so he allowed them to experience the implications of their foolish choices.

As Paul later wrote in the book of Galatians, "Do not be deceived; God is not mocked, for whatever one sows, that will he also reap (Gal 6:7)." The principle is clear: with proper care, the seeds we put in the ground will yield the intended produce. After all, if we planted corn, we would be stunned to go to our field and discover watermelons instead.

Likewise, God says that life produces similar results. Your actions will produce certain consequences in the same way that a seed produces a certain type of crop. Sometimes this process of sowing and reaping will be clear, public, and immediate. For example, a husband who consistently engages in an adulterous affair is likely to face the consequences of a broken marriage: wounded children and great pain to family and friends. However, there may be a time when the husband seems to get away with it. He is not caught and finds great joy through indulging the passions of his flesh. The internal consequences that no one sees may be just as real—shame over his actions, guilt over the implications for others, lack of peace with himself and God, and an inability to worship God joyfully and wholeheartedly. Internally and externally, the man is reaping what he sows.

The same process results from the types of sins we often assume are minor. Those who sow pride will reap broken relationships. Those who sow gossip will reap distrust. Those who sow worry will reap unbelief and waste God-given opportunities. Those who sow prayerlessness will miss out on reaping many answered prayers.

> *Jesus' sacrifice dealt with the curse and consequences of sin for the people who believe in him.*

> *The connection between sowing and reaping is an act of God's love.*

The connection between sowing and reaping is an act of God's love. The fruits we reap are meant to alert us to our foolish choices. Bad seeds produce bad fruit. We should feel conviction for our sin when we assess the field of our lives and find shame, guilt, broken relationships, distrust, or unbelief. The bad fruit we reap should drive us back to God in contrite repentance.

God has another motive for allowing us to reap the consequences of our actions. God acts to protect the honor of his name. He is unwilling to allow his people to mock his name in full view of a watching world. He has given his name to his people. Those who wear that name have a great responsibility to honor that name before those who do not yet believe. Christians must live in such a way that unbelievers will respond to the glory of God (1 Pet 2:9–12).

This was God's motive for kicking his people out of the land. It is also his motive in bringing them back from exile much later. The prophet Ezekiel, ministering during a time when many Jews were exiles in Babylon, writes,

> Therefore say to the house of Israel, Thus says the Lord GOD: It is not for your sake, O house of Israel, that I am about to act, but for the sake of my holy name, which you have profaned among the nations to which you came. And I will vindicate the holiness of my great name, which has been profaned among the nations, and which you have profaned among them. And the nations will know that I am the LORD, declares the Lord GOD, when through you I vindicate my holiness before their eyes. I will take you from the nations and gather you from all the countries and bring you into your own land (Ezek 36:22–24).

God acts to protect his name. He promised to bring the exiles back into the land in order to show the greatness of his name among the nations. God was concerned that the nations would doubt his greatness when they observed the scattered and fledgling group of Israelites in exile. Therefore, God would bring them back to the land and once again dwell there among them. God did this because of his great grace; not because his people deserved it.

God does the same for his people today. Those who are genuinely converted can trust that God is working to honor his name through their sowing and reaping. He will do this, at times, by allowing them to feel the consequences of their actions in order to draw them to repentance. Then, he will also lavish grace upon undeserving people to reveal his greatness to the world!

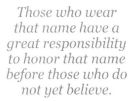

Those who wear that name have a great responsibility to honor that name before those who do not yet believe.

Food for Thought What are you currently reaping in your life? Is it the fruit of the Spirit—love, joy, peace, patience, kindness, goodness, faithfulness, gentleness, and self-control (Gal 5:22–23)? If not, consider the daily decisions you are making, particularly in areas that you might think are insignificant, and assess whether there is a direct connection between the fruits you are reaping and the choices you are sowing.

Make a list of the daily choices you face where you know you will choose between honoring **Faith in Action** God or not. Your list may include whether or not you spend time in prayer, gather with the church for worship, share your faith with your co-worker, or pray with your wife. Beside each choice you know you will make, consider what you would reap for each action. Obediently sharing your faith may produce confidence in God or joy in seeing someone come to faith. Failure to share your faith may lead to guilt or doubt in God's ability to use you for his mission in the world. Allow the process of sowing and reaping to reinforce your desire to obey God today.

Prayer

Thank God for not allowing you to get away with your sin. Praise him for his love and kindness that doesn't just let you do whatever you want to do. Worship him for pursuing you and loving you enough to correct your sinful heart.

The Dwelling of God

Deuteronomy 12:8–14

But when you go over the Jordan and live in the land that the LORD your God is giving you to inherit, and when he gives you rest from all your enemies around, so that you live in safety, then to the place that the LORD your God will choose, to make his name dwell there, there you shall bring all that I command you: your burnt offerings and your sacrifices, your tithes and the contribution that you present, and all your finest vow offerings that you vow to the LORD.
Deuteronomy 12:10–11

The first time someone moves into their own place—whether it is a dorm room, an apartment, or a house—they begin to make it their own. The previous owner's tastes in décor, paint color, or room layout are no longer important. A new owner has come, and what's inside will change based upon tastes of the latest resident. Depending on one's taste, they may remove the 80's retro vinyl wallpaper and go with a more modern dolphin grey eggshell paint for the living room. The pink ceramic tiles in the bathroom may give way to a . . . well pretty much anything is better than pink ceramic tiles, right? Over time, the home begins to look like the resident.

> *The promised land, while not a physical home, was the dwelling place God made for his people.*

God's people, in the book of Deuteronomy, are about to move into the greatest residence they could imagine. In fact, they had been imaging it for about 40 years. The promised land, while not a physical home, was the dwelling place God made for his people. It was a good place, filled with ample provision from the Lord. There, the people were to worship God, enjoy his favor, and live in peace.

They would dwell in the land in worshipful rest, Moses writes, because of another type of dwelling. It was not just that the people would dwell in the land, but that God would dwell with the people. God's dwelling with the people was more important than their dwelling in the land. The dwelling of God among the people was what made the land special in the first place. This was not the first time that God had taken residence among his people. He graciously chose to dwell among them in the tabernacle as they moved throughout the wilderness (Ex 29:45). A cloud in the day and a pillar of fire in the night reminded the people that God was with them (Ex 40:34).

But now God dwelt among them in a permanent location. Moses told the people that God would chose a location and there he would make his name dwell (12:11). At that location, God would accept the worship of his people (12:12).

This is another example of the astounding humility and grace of God. The sin-infested nation would have God live with them in the land. We would all likely be overwhelmed if our favorite athlete, movie-star, politician, or band decided to live with us. Or, more exactly, if our heroes built a house in the ritzy part of the best city in the world and invited us to come and live with them. This is what God was doing with his people. He designed the land especially for them, chose it as his dwelling, and invited the people to live with him there.

God wanted to dwell in the land among the people in such a way that everyone would know that God was the owner of the land. The ethical obedience of his people would be a primary way this would happen (Ex 19:5–6). The behavior of Israel was meant to distinguish them from the surrounding nations and prompt the curiosity of

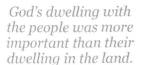

God's dwelling with the people was more important than their dwelling in the land.

the onlookers. Israel should have been astounded by the fact that God would dwell among them. They'd ask, "what great nation is there that has a god so near to it that the LORD our God is to us, whenever we call upon him" (Deut 4:7)?

The worship of God would be another primary way that God would mark his dwelling place (Deut 12:11). The tabernacle and the ongoing practice of sacrifice would be the epicenter of God's dwelling. There he would forgive sins and have fellowship with his people. The people could draw near to God because he had graciously drawn near to them.

John used similar language to speak of the sending of Jesus: "The Word became flesh and dwelt among us, and we have seen his glory, glory as of the only Son from the Father, full of grace and truth" (Jn 1:14). In Jesus, God dwelt among his people in the flesh. His followers, like the nation of Israel, were changed because he dwelt among them.

Following his death, burial, resurrection, and ascension, he then sent his Spirit—not simply to dwell among his people, but to live within them (Rom 8:9). The indwelling Spirit would mark God's people and transform all those in whom he resides.

The people could draw near to God because he had graciously drawn near to them.

The dwelling of God through his Spirit was the basis on which

93

> *If you are a Christian, God dwells in you by his Spirit as well.*

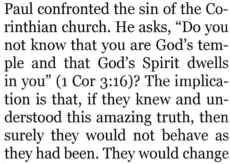

Paul confronted the sin of the Corinthian church. He asks, "Do you not know that you are God's temple and that God's Spirit dwells in you" (1 Cor 3:16)? The implication is that, if they knew and understood this amazing truth, then surely they would not behave as they had been. They would change because God dwells in them.

If you are a Christian, God dwells in you by his Spirit as well. The King of the Universe willingly makes his home in you. This is not because you are a worthy dwelling place for such an honored guest. Quite the opposite is the case. God chooses to dwell in his children and, from the inside out, makes changes to his dwelling place. Your life will be a massive construction project, where your new owner will bring his dwelling into conformity with his nature and character. To do this, he will have to demolish sin and rebuild your thoughts, actions, and affections so they model his holy character (1 Cor 3:17). This work will not be quick or easy, but it will be necessary. We can take heart, knowing that however difficult the transformation process, our owner is trustworthy, and we have the glorious privilege of being the dwelling place of God on earth.

Food for Thought What would change about your life if you lived with the conscious awareness that the Spirit of God lives within you? Paul exhorts the church to flee from sexual immorality for this reason (1 Cor 6:19–20). God's people must avoid sexual sin because God dwells within them. Thus, they should honor him with their bodies. How are you doing in this area of obedience? What needs to change about your behavior—particular in areas of sexual sin—in order to honor the dwelling of God properly in your life?

Faith in Action

Look around your house and find your favorite decoration or the one that best portrays your personality. In order to remind yourself of the dwelling of God, post the verse from 1 Corinthians 3:16 on that item. Every time you look at it, consider the dwelling of God in your life.

Prayer

Thank God for his willingness to dwell in someone like you. Ask him to increase your awareness of his presence on a daily basis and, as he does, to convict you of sin and continue the good work of transformation in your life.

In and Out

Deuteronomy 13:4–5

You shall walk after the LORD your God and fear
him and keep his commandments and obey his voice,
and you shall serve him and hold fast to him. But that
prophet or that dreamer of dreams shall be put to death,
because he has taught rebellion against the LORD your
God, who brought you out of the land of Egypt and
redeemed you out of the house of slavery, to make you
leave the way in which the LORD your God commanded
you to walk. So you shall purge the evil.
Deuteronomy 13:4–5

Physical life is impossible without breathing. The rhythmic process of inhaling and exhaling is a sure sign of life. Distance runners diligently train to control their breathing, knowing that their oxygen flow is essential in order to sustain a long run. Tiny babies are sent home with mommy and daddy when it is clear that they are breathing well on their own. At the other end of life, elderly residents of a nursing home, whose health is waning, may require oxygen tanks to make their way from one room to another. With each breath, living beings inhale life-giving oxygen and exhale carbon dioxide.

Spiritual life functions in much the same way. Christians inhale the life-giving truth of God's Word, found in the Holy Scriptures, and allow God's Spirit to make his truth clear, captivate hearts with God's glory, convict of

> God's people inhale the life-giving power of God's Spirit and exhale all forms of idolatry and wickedness.

known sin, and bring transformation (Heb 4:12). The Spirit, who already lives in believers, fills them with his power as they inhale God's good graces through the Word, prayer, fellowship with believers, corporate worship, the Lord's Supper, fasting, and other practices that God gives his church.

But exhaling is also critical. Physically, if you do not exhale properly, your lungs will fill with carbon dioxide, causing shallow breathing, a loss of breath, and an inability to take in the oxygen the body needs most. Exhaling poorly pollutes the body. Spiritually, if you do not exhale, you will suffer.

Throughout the book of Deuteronomy, Moses reminded the people of the need to inhale God's Word (6:4–9). In chapter 13, he reminded them of the need to exhale. Specifically, in this passage, he commands them to take drastic action against false prophets who dwell among them. God knew that these "dreamers of dreams" would contaminate the people—causing them to doubt God's Word and leading them astray. These evildoers should be destroyed, completely purging the nation of their destructive influence (13:4). This paradigm was not limited to false prophets—God also instructed the people to destroy all forms of idolatrous worship. Once they entered the land, Moses told the people to tear down the altars and burn the pillars used to worship false gods. "You shall chop down the carved images of their gods," Moses commands, "and destroy their name out of that place" (12:3).

God's people inhale the life-giving power of God's Spirit and exhale all forms of idolatry

> Lurking around every corner are temptations to self-sufficiency, pride, sexual immorality, consumerism, and a host of other gods of this age.

and wickedness. We do not do this naturally, however. Before salvation we were trapped in the fallen pattern of this world—incapable of extracting ourselves from its evil snare (Eph 2:1–3). After conversion, though we have the power to fight sin, we conform to the pattern of this world far too often (Rom 12:1–2). Our world is littered with idolatry rivaling the pagan practices of the nations surrounding Israel. Lurking around every corner are temptations to self-sufficiency, pride, sexual immorality, consumerism, and a host of other gods of this age. Like barnacles on the hull of a ship, we find the sinful patterns of this world attaching themselves to our lives in our thoughts, emotions, and actions.

Jesus instructed his followers to take drastic measures to rid themselves of evil. In his famous Sermon on the Mount, Jesus tied obedience to the desires of the heart. External acts such as murder and adultery, sprang to life due to hatred and lust in the human heart. Such evil must be ruthlessly purged from the heart of those who understand and respond to the grace of God. Jesus said:

> If your right eye causes you to sin, tear it out and throw it away. For it is better that you lose one of your members than that your whole body be thrown into hell. And if your right hand causes you to sin, cut it off and throw it away. For it is better that you lose one of your members than that your whole body go into hell (Mt 5:29–30).

Tear it out. Cut it off. Throw it away. Christians purge evil from their midst by relentlessly assessing their hearts, recognizing areas of disobedience, repenting before a holy God, and doing whatever is necessary to remove the sin they find.

Christians purge evil from their midst by relentlessly assessing their hearts, recognizing areas of disobedience, repenting before a holy God, and doing whatever is necessary to remove the sin they find.

Every person will purge evil in different ways. The college guy who consistently falls to pornography may need to give up his smartphone in exchange for an old-school, "dumb phone." He may need to get rid of his laptop and force himself to work in a public computer lab or the library. A lady struggling with doubt and anxiety may need to eliminate her constant, voyeuristic social media engagement that causes her to compare herself to others who seem to have it all together. The dad who is always too busy to spend quality time with his family may need to turn down the latest promotion or consider a job change in order to spend less time on the road. The actions will differ, but the process will not. God's people breathe in God's grace and breathe out anything that distorts or detracts from worshiping him as he deserves.

Food for Thought If you have walked with Jesus for any length of time, you have likely noticed certain repetitive sin issues in your life. Be it pride, worry, fear, lust, or anger—evil clings closely to our hearts. In this area, consider how you may need to exhale evil. Instead of rationalizing your lack of obedience, discern an appropriate step you could take to purge evil from your life.

Faith in Action

Fasting does not have to be limited to food alone. We can also fast from those behaviors that often produce evil in our lives. If you notice a certain activity or action often leads to sin, consider removing it for a time. TV, social media, or certain music may be first on the list. Commit to a certain time frame and tell a trusteed friend what you plan to do. Take note of how God uses this action to change your heart.

Prayer

Thank God that he has paid the price for evil through Jesus. Ask him to expose the way you continue to coddle the evil Jesus died to kill forever. Pray that he would prompt you to purge evil from your life today.

God's Solution to Poverty

Deuteronomy 15:4–5

*But there will be no poor among you; for the LORD will
bless you in the land that the LORD your God is giving
you for an inheritance to possess—if only you
will strictly obey the voice of the LORD your God,
being careful to do all this commandment that I
command you today.
Deuteronomy 15:4–5*

There's one like it in every city. In my hometown, the
place was called Blackmon Road. Located in a dilapidated
part of the city, Blackmon Road was final resting place for
the school district's discarded school buses. These buses
soon become home to the poor, who created a makeshift
community within this bus graveyard.

One Christmas, our family, along with other members of our local church, took bicycles to the children who
lived in this impoverished community. I was astounded at
the deplorable conditions these people lived in each day
while I lived with all of my needs met—and most of my
wants.

Poverty is a crippling reality for many around the
world. The simple fact that you and I can hold this book
and read the words it contains reveals our relative wealth

> **God cares about the poor.**

in comparison to the majority of the world's population. Politicians, business leaders, and seemingly everyone on social media banters about the best plan to alleviate poverty and care for those suffering under its weight.

God cares about the poor, too. Jesus told his followers that there would always be poverty in the world (Mt 26:11), yet God did not turn his back on these image-bearers. He is attentive to their needs, hears their prayers, and pursues them in his love (Ps 34:6).

The primary way God cares for the poor is through the sacrificial generosity of his people. At the heart of the law was the command for Israel to love their neighbor (Lev 19:18). This love extended beyond the borders of Israel, though. They were also to love to foreigners who lived within their land, seeing to it that they received the blessings afforded to God's people (Lev 19:33). God, through Moses, reminded the people that they were once foreigners in the land of Egypt and God cared for them. They should now do the same for others.

God established various regulations to ensure that Israel did not forget about the poor. For example, when an Israelite would glean from his fields, he was commanded to leave the food at the edges of the field for the poor and the foreigner. Rather than gathering one hundred percent of the harvest, the people of God would leave a portion in the fields so those in need could harvest what they needed to survive. This law of gleaning ensured that the poor were not neglected.

The Sabbath principle outlined by Moses in Deuteronomy chapter 15 had the same goal in mind. Every seven years, God's people were to cancel the debts of their fellow Israelites (15:1–2). God protected his people from economic exploitation and a widening gap between the haves and the have-nots (15:3).

Foreigners were expected to pay their debts, even in the Sabbath year. However, God's people must see to it that there were no poor among them (15:4). The economic release produced by the Sabbath principle would allow Israelites ample financial freedom to ensure that poverty was alleviated.

Because God cared for them, they were to care for others.

Physically, the people were meant to rest each Sabbath day, and, economically, they would rest each Sabbath year.

Moses once again reminded the people of God's care for them and his gracious gift of the land, lest the people doubt God's faithfulness (15:4). God was faithful to give them a land they did not deserve, and he would certainly provide for their needs, as they were obedient to care for others, they revealed their trust in God's continued provision for them. Because God cared for them, they were to care for others.

This principle extends into the New Testament church as well. Luke provides a compelling picture of the life of the church in Acts 2: "And all who believed were together and had all things in common. And they were selling their possessions and belongings and distributing the proceeds to all, as any had need" (Acts 2:44–45). God, once again, cared for the poor through the generosity of God's people.

Abundant wealth is not a prerequisite for extravagant generosity. The apostle Paul often spoke of the need

Abundant wealth is not a prerequisite for extravagant generosity.

for giving among the churches he established. The church in Macedonia was exceptional in their generosity and Paul saw to it that the church in Corinth took notice. Writing about this church, Paul said, "for in a severe test of affliction, their abundance of joy and

> *God's people give—
> it's just what they do.*

their extreme poverty have over-flowed in a wealth of generosity on their part. For they gave according to their means, as I can testify, and beyond their means, of their own accord, begin us earnestly for the favor of taking part in the relief of the saints" (2 Cor 8:2–4; emphasis mine). A famine prompted crip-pling poverty among many in Paul's day, and he often en-couraged his churches to give so that others' needs could be met. The Macedonian churches clearly understood their solidarity with their brothers and sisters in Christ in other cities. These churches were poor—extremely poor, yet Paul says they were begging to give.

God's people give—it's just what they do. The pri-mary objective for Christians should not be a minimal tip toward God's work on Sunday mornings when the offering is collected, nor should it be simply a standard percent-age given without thought or intentionality. We follow the model of a self-giving God and seek every opportunity to extend generosity to others.

Caring for all of God's image-bearers is the goal. The hope for the poor does not rest in the policy of a gov-ernment leader, but in the living service of God's church. We can live with intentionality to see to it that the needs of those around us are met. Through our giving, we mod-el the love of God and position ourselves to proclaim the gospel of Jesus. You don't have to look far to find a place to begin. Whether it's your city's version of Blackmon Road or a neighbor going through a hard time—find a tangible way to give to meet others' needs. Through these acts of giving, you will find that it is truly more blessed to give than to receive (Acts 20:35).

Food for Thought How do you typically respond to the poor? We can all do something, even though no one, in their own power, can alleviate all of the poverty in the world. God's people must prayerful discern how they can intentionally involve themselves in this vital work. We can, and should, do more than simply hand a few dollars through the car window in a crowded parking lot. What is God calling you to do this week?

The best place to begin is within your local church community Paul writes, "as we have **Faith in Action** opportunity, let us do good to everyone, and especially to those who are of the household of faith" (Gal 6:10). Membership in a local church community allows you to form family bonds with brothers and sisters in Christ. Often, within this community, needs will be known and burdens shared. Begin there and consider one tangible step you can take to ensure that the poor are cared for in your local church.

Prayer

Before God, acknowledge that everything you have comes from his hands. Thank him for the evidence of his kindness you notice in your life. Ask him to reveal ways that you can live with an open hand and allow others to experience God's kindness through your generosity.

Remember and Celebrate

Deuteronomy 16:1–8

*Observe the month of Abib and keep the Passover to the
LORD your God, for in the month of Abib the LORD your
God brought you out of Egypt by night. And you shall
offer the Passover sacrifice to the LORD your God, from
the flock or the herd, at the place that the LORD will
choose, to make his name dwell there.*
Deuteronomy 16:1–2

Christmas fills our minds with nostalgia as we reflect on traditions surrounding our celebration of Christ's
birth. One common, worldwide practice is the giving of
gifts. Gift giving is fraught with complexity —how do you
resist the siren call of materialism and consumerism? How
do you maintain a focus on Christ's birth? How do you get
the right gift for that person who has it all? Why do you
buy your child a gift when he would be satisfied with the
box? One common guide for parental gift giving encourag-
es parents to buy four gifts that fit these qualifications:
Something the child wants;
Something the child needs;
Something the child wears;
Something the child reads.

> *The institution of the Passover in Deuteronomy 16 is meant to remind the people of glorious nature of a gift giving God.*

I'm not sure my parents followed this paradigm, but in all honesty, I think I would have hated gifts based on that list when I was a child! Once I get past something I want, I lose interest—something I wear, really? Something to read—that sounds like a lot of work when I have a break from school. And something I need? Come on, now. That's a bit like saying, "Hey kid, we're going to the dentist on Christmas morning."

This doesn't have to be the case, however, if the person really knows you. If they know you have a genuine need, like jeans with holes in them, then this gift can be the most valuable of all. The remote control car will likely be crushed in two weeks, but not so with a gift that meets a real need.

Now, if the person doesn't know you well, you are in trouble. If your parents just relay a message to Great Aunt Gertrude saying that you need some new clothes, you might as well get your fake smile ready now. You might get a pair tube socks, or a coyote sweater designed with puff paint. They don't really know you, so they can't meet your need. For years to come, that coyote will accompany you to ugly sweater parties and live on as a testimony to the failure of sweet Gertrude.

The institution of the Passover in Deuteronomy 16 is meant to remind the people of glorious nature of a gift giving God—One who truly knows what people need. Let's assume for a moment that the God of the Bible exists. Some readers may doubt or deny this claim, but for argument's sake, let's assume that there is a God who created all things. He fashioned the world, everything you see, by the power of his Word. As the encore of his

> *The Passover was a foretaste of this coming salvation.*

creation handiwork, he made humans—intricately knitting them together in their mothers' wombs (Ps 139:19). Humans alone reflect the image of God to the world (Gen 1:26–28). Though these people who rebel from him and sin, he had a plan for bringing them back into a right relationship with himself.

> *The Lord's Supper provides another act that reminds the church of their need for God's grace and the glorious provision of Jesus Christ.*

The Passover was a foretaste of this coming salvation. God saved his people from death because of the blood sacrifice of a substitute, whose blood was plastered above their door (Ex 12:1–28). Each year, the people would gather to celebrate the Passover, and, each time, they would remember that their salvation was a gift from God and was only possible because of the death of a substitute. The people would offer a sacrifice to God as they called to mind the coming, promised sacrifice who would, once-and-for-all, pay the price for human sin (Heb 10:1–18). The Feast of Weeks (v. 9–12), the Feast of Booths (v. 13–17), and Israel's other national celebrations were meant to flood the people's hearts with nostalgia as they reflected on God's kindness to them.

National celebrations were not optional for the people. God commanded the festivals because they forced the people to remember his grace, leading them to worship him with glad hearts. God's people were a joyful people because their God was a gift-giving God.

> *The Lord's Supper eclipses the beauty of the Passover celebration—in fact Jesus' death was the very act to which the Passover pointed.*

These regular times of celebration and reminders continue to be vital for God's people. The weekly gathering of Christians in local churches provides one such time. Each week, God's people are reminded of their need for the grace of God through the preaching of the Scriptures, the prayers of the saints, the singing of the congregation, and the fellowship with brothers and sisters in Christ. The author of Hebrews reminded the church that these times must not be neglected because they are a chief catalyst for our growth in Christlikeness (Heb 10:24–25).

The Lord's Supper provides another act that reminds the church of their need for God's grace and the glorious provision of Jesus Christ. In this act instituted by Jesus, his broken body and spilt blood are symbolically given to those who, by grace through faith, have accepted his offer of salvation (1 Cor 11:17–34). The Lord's Supper eclipses the beauty of the Passover celebration—in fact Jesus' death was the very act to which the Passover pointed. Jesus was a perfect sacrifice whose singular act of substitution provided atonement for all of God's people. Each time we hold the broken bread and cup we affirm that God saw our need, acted on our behalf, and accomplished our salvation. The weekly gathering of the church and the celebration of the Lord's Supper serve to remind God's people that Jesus is all we truly need.

Food for Thought Do you prioritize time with God's people and the celebration of the Lord's Supper? In an action-packed world filled with full calendars it is easy to take these celebrations for granted. These acts are not arbitrary optional for an otherwise self-sufficient people. God graciously instituted them, and he commands that they be taken seriously.

Faith in Action

Spend time this week preparing for the corporate gathering of the church. Slow down on Saturday night, get plenty of rest, and ask God to give you a hunger to hear from him the next morning. Get up early on Sunday morning, arrive in plenty of time, and joyfully worship with God's people, expectantly believing that he will speak to you.

Prayer

Thank God that he knows your needs better than you do. Ask him to produce a profound sense of thankfulness and joy as you reflect on his grace through Christ.

Because He Said So

Deuteronomy 18:15–22

*I will raise up for them a prophet like you from among
their brothers. And I will put my words in his mouth,
and he shall speak to them all that I command him.*
Deuteronomy 18:18

Parents are notorious for the quip, "because I said
so." These four words are the go-to parenting response for
the incessant questions their children ask. "Because I said
so" is also parental code for, "I'm so tired I can barely think
straight and, though I don't have a clear reason, my sanity
depends on you obeying me right now."

If anyone has the right to make this statement, it
is God. He is God, after all. As the ruler over Creation, he
has the right to command everything he created to obey
him. These commands for obedience, though, are rooted
in his love for his people and his knowledge of what is truly
in their best interest. Unlike parents, every one of God's
commands is motivated by pure intentions and designed
for the good of his people.

The middle section of the book of Deuteronomy
is filled with a host of miscellaneous laws that, if obeyed,
would mark Israel as God's holy people. Laws concerning
justice (16:18–20), the prosecution of evildoers (17:1–7),

> *Every one of God's commands is motivated by pure intentions and designed for the good of his people.*

legal decisions (17:8–13), the appointment of kings (17:14–20), provision for the priestly Levites (18:1–8), the destruction of the pagan practices of the nations (18:9–14), cities of Refuge for the accused (19:1–13), military strategy and warfare (20), marriage (21:10–14), and a myriad of other laws (22:1–12). Many of these laws may seem antiquated and cryptic to a modern reader. Yet, God commanded his people to obey because he was God and he knew what was best for his people.

Often, God did not speak to them directly, but he spoke to them through a prophet (like Moses) who would hear from God and communicate his message to the people. Moses served as a mediator between God and the nation, even though he was unable to enter the promised land due to his sin. God instructed the people that, following Moses' death, he would continue to raise up prophets after him who would bring his word to the people.

Once they entered the land, God would use certain prophets to warn the people of God's judgment if they continued to live in rebellion. They did not heed these warnings, and, in time, both the northern kingdom and the southern kingdom were sent into exile. The Assyrians sacked the northern kingdom in 722 BC and deported many Israelites. Soon thereafter, the Babylonians claimed the southern kingdom in 598 BC. Prophets continued to speak the Word of God to his people—though they were now scattered among the nations. In time, a remnant of the nation returned to the promised land and began to rebuild the temple and the city walls. They, too, heard the Word of God from the prophets, who spoke of God's continued hatred

> *Jesus could do what the prophets could not do; he could perfectly obey the very Word he proclaimed.*

of evil and the hope of the coming Messiah.

God used the prophets to communicate to his people, but they could not save the people. The nation was incapable of heeding the prophetic warnings, and continued toward their impending destruction. God continued to ful-

Jesus says, "I am God. Do this because I say so."

fill the promise of Deuteronomy 18 in the person of Jesus. The author of Hebrews wrote, "Long ago, at many times and in many ways, God spoke to our fathers by the prophets, but in these last days he has spoken to us by his Son, whom he appointed the heir of all things, through whom he created the world" (Heb 1:1–2). The speaking God continued to speak through Jesus—the Word made flesh who made his dwelling among the people (John 1:1–14). He proclaimed the Word of God to the people, inviting them into his kingdom through faith and repentance (Mt 3:2). Jesus could do what the prophets could not do; he could perfectly obey the very Word he proclaimed. Because Jesus was the exact imprint of the nature of God, people could see the God's Word when they observed the life of Christ (Heb 1:3). He could command people to do what he said and do what he did. Jesus was God's perfect prophet.

As God, he had the authority to command his followers to obey his Word. At the end of his life, Jesus gave his disciples his famous Great Commission. Jesus introduced this commission with these words: "All authority in heaven and on earth has been given to me" (Mt 28:18). Before commanding them to make disciples, baptize converts, and teach people to obey, Jesus reminded them of his authority. In effect, Jesus says, "I am God. Do this because I say so." And, he has every right to command them to obey because

Obedience to God demonstrates a humble respect for his authority and is an indelible mark of the Christian life.

he has all authority—not only on earth but also in heaven. His authority also extends to all people because he fashioned every man, woman, and child in his image. As their creator, he has authority over their lives as well.

The same authority lies behind all of Jesus' commandments. We hear the Word of God because he said so, and we should obey the Word for the very same reason—because he is God and he said so. Obedience to God demonstrates a humble respect for his authority and is an indelible mark of the Christian life.

Food for Thought

What aspects of life are you most prone to question or deny God's authority? Consider aspects of life such as marriage, giving, evangelism, or faithfulness to the spiritual disciplines. Why do you fail to submit to God's authority in this area?

Faith in Action

God continues to speak to his people through his Son. The clear path to seeing the Son and, thus, to hearing from God is to spend consistent time in God's Word. You are on a good path as you work through the book of Deuteronomy in this study. Take time now to develop a plan for how you will carve out consistent time in the Word once you finish this study.

Prayer

Thank God that he is not an arbitrary dictator but a loving ruler, who knows what is best for his people and commands them to obey. Confess your pride and lack of submission and ask him to overwhelm you with a sense of his power and authority.

A Temple of the Living God

Deuteronomy 22:13–30

If a man is found lying with the wife of another man,
both of them shall die, the man who lay with the woman,
and the woman. So you shall purge the evil from Israel.
Deuteronomy 22:22

Our world is a minefield of sexual perversion. With each passing moment, people face temptations that can destroy their lives in one fatal step. The pornographic culture of modern America is nothing new. Throughout human history, all cultures have evidenced the diabolical nature of sexual immorality. Certain cultures at specific stages of history have fostered this sin in differing ways. For example, the advent of the modern technological era filled homes with pornography with a mere click. The ancient Jewish world was filled with different, though no less destructive, forms of sexual perversion.

Sex is created by God and designed for his glory and our good, but the Fall twists, distorts, and mars his good gift (Gen 1:28). The warnings given by Moses reveal just how far humanity fell. From verses 13 to 30, Moses describes differing types of sexual sin and lists the corresponding punishment for each. Two facts are clear from this list.

> *The pervasive presence of sexual sin means that God's people must always be on their guard.*

First, sexual sin is pervasive. Moses addressed some familiar types of sexual immorality—such as rape and adultery—because these acts would plague the nation as they entered the land. Moses must single out these sins and speak to them at length because he knew the people were prone to rebel from God in these ways. The sinister grip of sexual deviance constricts around all people, albeit in differing ways at differing times. In fact, sexual sin is one of the base forms of idolatry because it represents an exchange of worship of Creator God for worship of created things—in this case, other people he has made. This idolatry is not limited to the two areas Moses addressed in this text, though. Idolatrous lust manifests itself in other ways as well, such as premarital sex, pornography, and homosexuality. The pervasive presence of sexual sin means that God's people must always be on their guard.

Second, sexual sin has consequences. The judgments listed by Moses likely seem harsh to the modern reader. Paying restitution, whipping, and stoning are startling ways of addressing such sin. Yet, Moses is clear that these drastic measures were necessary in order to "purge evil from your midst" (Deut 22:21, 22, 24). It is clear that God is serious about sexual perversion. We cannot simply wink at such sin and hide behind the excuse "Well, everyone is doing it." Sexual sin incurs the judgment of God, and, for this reason, God's people must not coddle it. They should ruthlessly eliminate it from their lives and from their community.

At first glance, it may seem that the severity of the consequences for sexual sin within the nation of Israel far exceeds the implications of sin in our day. We are certainly not likely to stone a young man who violates the purity of a virgin or kill a man who engages in an extramarital affair. However, these sins have disastrous consequences nonetheless. A young woman who frivolously gives herself to any man who will pay her attention will find deadening consequences to her physical, emotional, and spiritual life. She will not escape unscathed. A man who habitually feasts on pornographic images will destroy his sense of beauty, sear his mind and conscience, and live with crippling shame and guilt. The college girl who spurns her parents' counsel and pursues a homosexual relationship will bring harm on herself, wound her parents, and distort God's plan for marriage. A couple that engages in an extramarital affair will destroy their marriages and do long-term harm to their friends, family, and children. The stakes are indeed high!

Moses instructed the people to purge the sexually immoral from the community. At this point in history, God dwelt among his people, the nation of Israel, in the tabernacle. His presence filled the community and was incompatible with sexual perversion.

Following the death, burial, and resurrection of Jesus, God dwells among his people in a different way. He sends his Spirit to live in his people and not merely among them (Acts 2:1–13). Not only that, but his Spirit does not simply fill Israelites, but lives within all those who trust in Christ's work. The Spirit of the living God can fill all people—those from differing nations, races, and socio-economic classes.

Paul used this logic to challenge the Corinthian church to avoid sexual sin (1 Cor 6:12–20). He reminded them that they were filled with God's Holy Spirit, and, for this reason, they should honor God with their bodies. Sexual sin takes a body filled with God's Spirit and engages it in flagrant immorality. He writes, "Or do you not know that your body is a temple of the Holy Spirit within you, whom you have form God? You are not your own, for you were bought with a price. So glorify God

Sexual sin takes a body filled with God's Spirit and engages it in flagrant immorality.

> *Sexual immorality is incompatible with the holiness of God's church.*

in your body" (1 Cor 6:19–20). Paul echoes Moses when he tells the church to purge those who do not heed his warning from their midst (1 Cor 5:13). Sexual immorality is incompatible with the holiness of God's church.

Paul gives a singular command for how the people of God should respond to sexual sin—"Flee from sexual immorality" (1 Cor 6:18). This begins on a personal level as God's people acknowledge, repent, and run from evil. Like Joseph and Potiphar's wife, those who love God seek to remove themselves from any kind of evil advance (Gen 39:12–13). This may mean ending an impure relationship, getting rid of a computer or smartphone riddled with pornography, confessing sin to a spouse, or repenting of flirtatious advances on social media.

Fleeing from sexual sin extends to the corporate level as well. Holiness should mark God's church as the individuals who make up the congregation pursue holiness. Believers, out of love for one another, must confront professing brothers or sisters in Christ who are living contrary to God's holiness. They must do so in love and with a tone of grace, but they must not allow sexual sin to go unchecked or unaddressed (Col 4:6). This will always begin with personal and private confrontation of sin, though, if this counsel is not heeded, it may need to be addressed by others in the church as well (Mt 18:15–20). Gossip and malicious slander are not fitting for God's people, but loving confrontation is not only acceptable—it is necessary in order to protect the church from the destructive implications of sexual sin. Unlike the nation of Israel, we have the full knowledge of the person and work of Jesus Christ, to motivate

> *We have the full knowledge of the person and work of Jesus Christ, to motivate our personal and corporate fight for holiness.*

our personal and corporate fight for holiness. And, in light of the glory of the gospel, we must fight indeed.

Food for Thought

Do you flee sexual sin? Only you can answer that question, because it is likely that you are the only one who knows the way in which your heart is prone to deception and failure in these areas. We are all prone to rationalize the foolish decisions we make and assume that these habits will just go away or that they are not really that bad in the first place. Allow God to convict you of such rationalization and force you to address your sin before it is too late.

Faith in Action

Sexual sin never affects only you. Particularly if you are dating, engaged, or married, your sin in these areas has massive implications, even if you don't see them right now. By God's grace, confess your sins to this person and ask them for forgiveness today.

Prayer

Thank God that his Spirit lives within you. Pray that he would heighten your awareness of this truth on a daily basis and that it would shape the decisions that you make—especially in the areas of sexual sin.

What God Joins Together

Deuteronomy 24:1–4

And you shall not bring sin upon the land that the LORD your God is giving you for an inheritance.
Deuteronomy 24:4

There are certain areas of life that you don't want to talk about with your extended family at the Thanksgiving dinner table. Immigration policy, the definition of marriage, international military strategy, and abortion are subjects that most would rather avoid. Conversation about these topics is likely to produce awkward conversation and, perhaps, a good argument. If you are a Christian, people may often want to know what the Bible teaches on these topics. Some answers are quite clear, while others are a bit more challenging.

The topic Moses broaches in chapter 24 is one such topic. Divorce is an issue that plagues our modern culture—with many marriages ending in divorce. This is, without question, contrary to God's design. He designed marriage as the final act in his masterful work of creation (Gen 2:18–25). He is the one who joins a man and a woman in a one-flesh union—one that no one should separate (Mk 10:9). These lasting, irrevocable marriages are meant

> *God's people must work to uphold a high view of marriage and do nothing to destroy what God has joined together.*

to portray God's unceasing, inalterable, unbreakable love for his people (Eph 5:22–33).

The epidemic of divorce forces us to consider the Bible's verdict on this topic. Moses addressed the topic at the end of lengthy section of commandments for God's people as they prepared to enter the promised land. His brief discussion of divorce is not designed to provide a holistic explanation of God's view on the topic, but merely to place increased restrictions on a practice that was common within the nation of Israel as well.

Thankfully, Jesus provides greater clarity on this passage in Matthew's Gospel. In chapter 19, Jesus is questioned regarding his position on marriage. Before addressing the specific situations that might prompt divorce, Jesus provided a summary statement regarding the institution of divorce. The following exchange between Jesus and the Pharisees is revealing:

"They said to him, 'Why then did Moses command one to give a certificate of divorce and to send her away?' He said to them, 'Because of your hardness of heart Moses allowed you to divorce your wives, but from the beginning it was not so'" (Mt 19:7–8). Jesus claimed that Moses' allowance of divorce was a concession for human sin. This was not his design, but it was instituted for the nation of Israel to address a problem that, if left unchecked, would cause even greater harm.

Jesus then addressed a specific siltation that often causes divorce—sexual sin. Evangelical scholars differ on their understanding of the statements that follow. Some hold that Jesus made an allowance for a biblical divorce if one partner was unfaithful in the marriage. In 1 Corinthians 7, Paul provided another possible allowance for divorce, desertion by an unbelieving spouse (1 Cor 7:15). Taken together, some believe that sexual immorality and desertion are the two situations in which divorce is acceptable.

This posture may obscure the greater truth taught by Jesus in this passage. Even if sexual sin and desertion are grounds for divorce, they still result from the hardness of the human heart. It should not be assumed that because they necessitate divorce that they make divorce desirable. At best, divorce is a legal concession for sinful humanity living in a sin-saturated world. It is interesting to note that Jesus' instructions regarding divorce come on the heels of his command to radical forgiveness (Mt 18:21–35).

God's people must work to uphold a high view of marriage and do nothing to destroy what God has joined together. For example, you may find yourself in the midst of a challenging marriage today. Rather than seeking an out, God's design is for you to fight for your marriage, pursue your spouse, forgive, and seek healing and restoration in your marriage. This may seem like an unrealistic goal in light of the complexity of marriage and the challenges it produces. But, be reminded, God understands exactly what it is like to be in a hard marriage. In fact, there has never been a harder marriage than his relationship to the church. The biblical authors commonly use the image of adultery to describe the sin of God's people (Isa 1:21; 50:1; 57:3; Jer 3:1–20; Eze 16:35–39; 23:1–49; James 4:4). Yet, God continually pursues his adulterous people and lovingly maintains his covenant promises to them. God's people, modeling his love, should do the same in their marriages. Even in the face of difficult marriages, God's people have a wonderful chance to model his love for his people and proclaim the beauty of the gospel message. In fact, it is in difficult marriages that this type of love is best portrayed.

> *God's design is for you to fight for your marriage, pursue your spouse, forgive, and seek healing and restoration in your marriage.*

We must also work to encourage those whom we love to fight for their marriages. Chris-

> *We must also work to encourage those whom we love to fight for their marriages.*

tians are a burden-bearing people (Gal 6:2). We can assume that every married couple in our churches is struggling through the trials that invariably come when someone seeks to love another sinner. The church should be a community where we pray for one another, fight for our marriages together, and seek to encourage and challenge each other to love our spouses with a Christ-honoring love.

Finally, many have already gone through the pain of divorce. Remember that God's grace is found these deep valleys of life (Ps 23). Though your divorce resulted from sin, God is sufficient to forgive sin and create a pure heart in you (Ps 51). Do not allow shame and guilt to cripple you or hinder God's good purposes for your life (Eph 2:10). If you are a Christian, you can be assured that "he who began a good work in you will bring it to completion at the day of Jesus Christ" (Phil 1:6). God is using every circumstance in your life, even your divorce, to accomplish his plan of conforming you to the image of Jesus (Rom 8:28–30). God can, and will, use your deepest pain to display his glory and bring about your transformation.

The grace of God compels God's people to fight for their marriages. We do not capitulate to cultural norms or sub-biblical rationale for pursuing our own sinful desires. Rather, by the grace of God and the power of his Spirit, we seek to display God's love in our marriages—even when this seems impossible, because with God all things are possible (Mt 19:26).

> *The church should be a community where we pray for one another, fight for our marriages together, and seek to encourage and challenge each other to love our spouses with a Christ-honoring love.*

Food for Thought

In what way has divorce impacted your life? You may have experienced divorce firsthand or grown up in a family broken by sin. Consider how God may use this pain to allow you to care for others and conform you to his image.

Faith in Action

Ongoing repentance is the best strategy for health in a marriage. We must seek to confess our sins to our spouse and seek restoration long before sin builds up a head of steam and destroys our lives. If you have been harboring sin, bitterness, or unforgiveness, acknowledge this to your spouse today and seek to model the love of Christ.

Prayer

Thank God for creating marriage to display his love for his people. If you are married, celebrate the gift of your spouse and ask God to continue to grow your capacity for love in this relationship. Also spend time praying for those who are struggling through broken marriages and relational failures. Ask God to do the impossible in these relationships and restore these marriages for their good and his glory.

The Blame Game

Deuteronomy 24:16

Fathers shall not be put to death because of their children, nor shall children be put to death because of their fathers. Each one shall be put to death for his own sin.
Deuteronomy 24:16

Decisions have consequences. If you throw a rock straight up into the air, it is likely to hit you in the head and leave you with an embarrassing scar. If you eat fast food for 10 straight days, you'll probably gain ten pounds and your stomach will hate you. Life is an outworking of the decisions we make each day.

Throughout Deuteronomy, Moses clearly established this principle. Paired with the miscellaneous laws that dominate the middle section of this book are descriptions of the consequences for disobedience. At the outset of chapter 25, Moses depicted the punishment for those found guilty in a court of law (vv. 1–4). These consequences were seen as an extension of the judgment of God and were meant to restrain others from indulging in the same practices.

Moses warned that only the evildoer is to be held responsible for his or her sins. A son is not complicit in his father's wickedness, nor is the father in his son's. Each person must be held accountable for his own sin and judged accordingly.

> *Life is an outworking of the decisions we make each day.*

This principle is particularly important because people are prone to blame others for their folly. After Adam and Eve sinned, they played the blame game (Gen 3). Rather than owning his sin and repenting of it, Adam blamed Eve for giving him the fruit. Then, Eve blamed the serpent for her deception.

Blame is one of the most common ways we respond to sin. A naïve teenager is likely to blame her friends if she misses her curfew and fails to check in with her parents. An addict may blame his family of origin or his genetic makeup for his consistent drunkenness. An adulterer may blame his waywardness on his wife's ambivalence towards. A Christian may blame her busyness or personality for her failure to share the gospel with those far from God. This finger pointing deflects personal responsibility for our sin and appeases our conscience—at least for a time.

Yet, we are all personally responsible for our sin before a holy God. As Moses wrote, "Each one shall be put to death for his own sin (24:16)." Of course, there are a host of factors that contribute to our actions. Children raised without a father are more likely to drop out of high school, engage in violent behavior, and end up in prison. Peer pressure shapes the actions of teenagers. Alcoholism contributes to anger. The sin of one person affects others—especially within the family. According to Moses, God will visit "the iniquity of the fathers on the children, to the third and the fourth generation (Num 14:18)." The implications of parental sin will have lasting implications on their children; this is an undeniable fact.

> *We are all personally responsible for our sin before a holy God.*

The sins of others is not the source of our own sin, however. We are personally responsible for the choices we make and the ways that we respond to the circumstances of our lives. And, according to the apostle Paul, "We must all appear before the judgment seat of Christ, so that each one may receive what is due for what he has done in the body, whether good or evil (2 Cor 5:10)." Again, Paul made this point to the church in Rome: "For we will all stand before the judgment seat of God; for it is written 'As I live, says the Lord, every knee shall bow to me, and every tongue shall confess to God. So then each of us will give an account of himself to God (Rom 14:10–12)." Because God is the true King and a just Judge, all people will give an account for their actions before him.

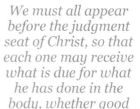

We must all appear before the judgment seat of Christ, so that each one may receive what is due for what he has done in the body, whether good or evil.

Thankfully, Christians will stand before God clothed in the righteous standing of Jesus Christ (Is 61:10; Zech 3:4). God gives the perfect life of Christ to believers by faith; therefore, they stand before him holy and pure. Still, this reality is a personal one. No one is right with God based on the faith of someone else. God does not grant access to heaven because our parents were Christians. We must each personally choose to repent of our sins and trust in Jesus' work in order to have confidence on the Day of Judgment.

A deadly fate awaits those who have not placed their faith in Christ. The death sentence given to evildoers in the book of Deuteronomy is a vivid reminder of the death sentence that awaits all those who reject God's offer of salvation (Mt 7:13–14; Lk 13:22–30). On that day, all people will give an account for their inability to keep God's law. For the first time, they will bow the knee

We must each personally choose to repent of our sins and trust in Jesus' work in order to have confidence on the Day of Judgment.

before the glory of God, but it will be too late. They will experience the condemnation of God because of their sin, their failure to accept God's offer of forgiveness, and their unwillingness to receive the gift of Christ's righteousness will result in their condemnation.

Each person's sin must be punished. Either the punishment will be credited to Jesus' work on the cross, or each person will pay for his or her sin—for all eternity. Today, you have a chance to trust in Jesus before it is too late. You may be prone to blame a variety of people or circumstances for your actions. Indeed, these factors may contribute to your behavior, but you alone are responsible for your sinful heart. Similarly, you alone can repent of your sinful life and trust in Jesus Christ for salvation. Do so today while there is still time.

Sin does have consequences on others. The fact that Christians are clothed in the righteousness of Christ does not mean that their sin does not matter. It does. Our actions, either good or bad, have a shaping effect on others—either in pointing them to Christ or away from him. Does your life have a positive or negative effect on those closest to you? Have you professed faith in Jesus Christ? If not, please pause to read "Finding L.I.F.E. in Jesus" at the end of this book. This is the most important decision of your life!

If you recognize that your sin has negatively effected someone else, seek to make that situation right today. Ask them for forgiveness, admit your need for the grace of God, and seek to change by the power of God.

If you are a Christian, thank God that you will never have to pay the price for you sin. Praise God for his kindness in taking the wrath that you deserve and clothing you in the perfect standing of Jesus. Pray for those you love—friends, family, neighbors, and coworkers—who do not know this hope. Ask God to reveal himself to them and change their hearts before the day when they will stand before his judgment seat and answer for their sins.

Giving Thanks: In All Circumstances

Deuteronomy 26:1–3

When you come into the land that the LORD your God is giving you for an inheritance and have taken possession of it and live in it, you shall take some of the first of all the fruit of the ground, which you harvest from your land that the LORD your God is giving you, and you shall put it in a basket, and you shall go to the place that the LORD your God will choose, to make his name to dwell there.
Deuteronomy 26:1–2

If you have ever traveled to a different culture (particularly to a place with a drastically different socio-economic level than your own), then you know the mental transformation that can result. It's one thing to know that poverty exists; it is another thing altogether to experience it firsthand. Local churches will send short-term missions teams to impoverished places around the world in the hopes of meeting their physical needs and sharing the hope of the gospel with them. Those who return from such trips will often say, "I never knew how good I had it until I saw the suffering of people around the world." Or, "I took so much for granted before I went on this trip."

> *We are not good at being thankful.*

These emotions expose an all-too-common reality about most of us: We are not good at being thankful. As Moses warned God's people, the abundance seen in many of our lives can produce a self-sufficiency that fosters forgetfulness of God favor and blindness to his good gifts in our lives. Wouldn't it be great if you and I could live with a spirit of thankfulness at all times and not just when we go on a mission trip or see someone else in need?

Moses' instructions in Deuteronomy 26 reminded the people of the necessity of thankfulness as they entered the land. After a lengthy summary regarding the outworking of the law (16:18–25:19), Moses reminded the people of one final act of obedience. In fact, this final act of obedience would allow an ancient Israelite to say that he had kept all of the law (26:13). Thankful, joyful, and abundant giving put an exclamation point on the obedience of the nation.

Of course, they had much for which to be thankful. God brought them into the land, gave them victory against their enemies, and allowed them to feast on his bountiful provision. He told them, though, that they had a responsibility to give thanks to God by offering some of the fruit of the land back to him in worship.

This may seem a bit strange—like kids buying their parents a Christmas gift with the parents' money. Why would God give it to them, only to ask for some of it back? And, why would God want it back anyway, since he is not hungry and in need of the produce? God commanded the people to give because this is the proper response to the grace of God. God gives, so his people

> *Wouldn't it be great if you and I could live with a spirit of thankfulness at all times and not just when we go on a mission trip or see someone else in need?*

should give also. He provides, so his people give thanks. Grace produces giving.

God was quite specific about the nature of this giving. He told them what they were to give: the fruit of the ground (v. 2). He told them when they were to give it: the first time they harvested (v.

God commanded the people to give because this is the proper response to the grace of God.

2). He instructed them as to how to package the offering: in a basket (v. 2). He commanded that they offer it to a specific person: the priest (v. 3). And, he even told them exactly what they were to say when they offered it (v. 3). God was not vague in his requirements; he told them exactly what they were to do.

At first glance, these commands seem incredibly rigid and ritualistic. We may be hesitant to apply responses like these to our own lives, because we may think that our worship would become sterile, rote, or mechanical. On the other hand, God knows far more about the human heart than we do. He knows that our affections will not drift toward thankfulness, so we must have an anchor for our feelings. Specific, intentional practices of thankfulness are vital for the worshipful obedience of the people of God—our feelings will not suffice. Sure, there may be times when we "feel" thankful, but there will also be many times when we feel burdened, discouraged, and apathetic. Unless we have an anchor for our feelings, we will naturally fail to give thanks to God consistently and joyfully.

Specific, intentional practices of thankfulness are vital for the worshipful obedience of the people of God—our feelings will not suffice.

Still, we may find ourselves being thankful from time to time. Occasional thanks, however, will be the reactive type. You know, the kind of thanks you feel when you are speeding down the interstate and you pass a cop hidden in the bushes. For the next two miles, you

> *Thankfulness based on circumstances is reactive. Thankfulness rooted in the nature and character of God is proactive.*

are fixated on your rearview mirror, hoping against hope that the cop was asleep or that the car next to you was going a bit faster than you were. "Thank God. He didn't stop me," may be your words if a few minutes pass, and you are not sitting shamefully on the side of the road with blue lights behind you.

Proactive thanksgiving is far more challenging. Daily intentional thanksgiving (regardless of the circumstance) should be the pattern for the Christian life. For this to happen, Moses challenged the people to make thankfulness a discipline in their lives. They were not to give thanks simply when they felt like it, but when God commanded it (and even if they didn't feel like it).

Unfortunately, many embrace the faulty logic that doing something that you don't feel like doing is bad or even wrong. We fear hypocrisy, and so we say, "Why would I fake it and do something that I don't feel like doing?" God knows that our feelings are a woefully inadequate guide for life. As a regular discipline, we must do things that we don't feel like doing in order to train our feelings regarding what is good, pure, lovely, and right.

The path to disciplined thankfulness is found in Deuteronomy 26:5-9. Moses recounted the story of God's faithfulness to his people. In spite of their folly, he saw fit to fulfill his promises and bring them into a good land. He saved them "with a mighty hand and an outstretched arm (v.8)." His actions, and not the circumstances of the people, were the basis for their thanks. It would be easy for the people to give thanks the first time they entered the land, but Moses knew that unless they developed the disciplined act of thanksgiving, rooted in God's faithfulness, they would never sustain a thankful heart for long.

Thankfulness based on circumstances is reactive. Thankfulness rooted in the nature and character of God is proactive. The consistency of God's character allows us to give thanks for what is to come and not just give thanks for the good things that happen.

Since God never changes, there is never a time when we cannot give thanks. Paul made this point in one of the most convicting passages in the entire Bible. He wrote, "Give thanks in all circumstances, for this is the will of God in Christ Jesus for you (1 Th 5:18)." Paul answered one of the most common questions asked by many Christians: "What is God's will for my life?" One other time, in 1 Thessalonians 4:3 Paul said, "For this is the will of God, your sanctification." In 1 Thessalonians 5, he said that the will of God is for Christians to give thanks. Thankfulness and sanctification are the will of God for all of his children. Yes, God's will may include a certain spouse or career, but we can be certain that God's will is thankfulness and sanctification.

Notice the nature of this thankfulness: it is "in all circumstances." And this includes the good and the bad; the hopeful seasons and the seasons of discouragement; the times of great joy and the times of great sorrow. The will of God is for you and me to give thanks in all of these circumstances. The only way we can do this is to root our thanksgiving "in Christ Jesus." In Christ, God has shown the abundance of his grace to us. Much more than a physical land, God has given his children in the church a glorious inheritance with him in heaven. He has brought his children from death to life. He has forgiven our sins! He has clothed us in the righteousness of Jesus! He is eternally pleased with us! For this, and much more, we should always give thanks.

Food for Thought

Do you practice the discipline of thankfulness? Odds are, unless you have an intentional practice that forces you to give thanks, you will quickly become forgetful. What times during the week to make a priority to give thanks?

Faith in Action

If you do not have a regular time of thanksgiving, make a plan for one today. What time during your week could you set aside to do nothing else but give God thanks? How could you plan times of thanksgiving into the rhythm of each day?

Prayer

Praise God for his grace in Christ Jesus. Begin by giving him thanks for his character and his work in Christ. Try to avoid basing your praise on your circumstances at this point. Discipline your thoughts to thankfulness based on what cannot be taken from you if your circumstances change.

Giving Thanks: Generous Worship

Deuteronomy 26:12–15

When you have finished paying all the tithe of your produce in the third year, which is the year of tithing, giving it to the Levite, the sojourner, the fatherless, and the widow, so that they may eat within your towns and be filled
Deuteronomy 26:12

Through Moses, God linked a number of critical concepts together throughout the book of Deuteronomy. One of these concepts is the necessity of humility for the people of God as they enter the land (see Day 6). The land was a gift, and in it they would find cities they did not build, cisterns they did not dig, and abundant food they did not plant (Deut 6:11). But, humility is difficult to gauge. How do you know if someone is humble? How do you know if you are?

As we saw yesterday, the answer is thankfulness. Giving thanks is the outward manifestation of a humble heart. Humble people are thankful, and thankful people stay humble.

Moses adds one final link in chapter 26. Not only does humility lead to thankfulness, but also thankfulness produces giving. Moses commanded the people of God to

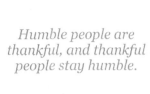

Humble people are thankful, and thankful people stay humble.

offer their thanks to him through tangible acts of giving. They were to give God the first fruits of the ground—a tithe of their resources (vv. 1–3, 12). The people of God were called to do more than merely feel thankful; they were called to give tangible gifts that demonstrated their thankfulness.

It may be helpful to view this as a progression from the heart to the hands. First, God's people should have a humble heart. These humble hearts should produce thankfulness in their minds. From humble hearts and thankful minds, they will use their hands to give.

Marriage provides a context to see this process at work. Every husband feels love for his wife in his heart (or at least he should). His love for his wife produces thankfulness for the ways she loves and serves. He calls to mind the ways she sacrifices each day to care for their home and meet the needs of their children. As a result, he gives graciously to her. He serves her in tangible ways to demonstrate through his actions the love and thankfulness he feels in his heart. He may vacuum the house, buy her a gift, plan a date night, or offer the supreme act of love—wash the dishes! When a humble heart meets a thankful mind, ones hands will produce external actions that reflect gratitude.

God's people give. In the nation of Israel, this active giving provided for the needs of the Levites, the priests of God They had no permanent portion of land and depended on the giving of the people to provide for their needs. In addition, this giving provided for the sojourner, the fatherless, and the widow among the Jews. Those burdened by the pains of life received God's blessings through the kindness of his people. These

God's people were not to be stingy in their giving.

people did not simply eat—they ate until they were full (26:12). God's people were not to be stingy in their giving. They gave and gave abundantly.

God's people give because God gave.

There are two primary motives God's people to give. First, and foremost, their giving is based on the self-giving nature of God himself. He gave them the land (26:1). More than that, he gave them himself. He revealed his covenant name to his people (Ex 3), chose them to be his treasured possession (Deut 7:6; 26:18), redeemed them from slavery in Egypt (Ex 14), gave them his Word (Ex 20), and filled them with his presence (Ex 13:21–22). God's people give because God gave.

The self-giving nature of God does not stop in the book of Deuteronomy, however. It gets better in the New Testament. God gave his greatest gift to his people in the person of Jesus Christ, his son, who willingly laid aside equality with God and assumed the form of a servant (Phil 2:6–11). Jesus' brutal execution was the supreme gift of God's love. Those who receive from Jesus the gifts of forgiveness of sin and eternal salvation respond by giving.

Second, God's mission in the world motivates God's people to give. The people marginalized and broken by life in a fallen world need to experience the grace God offers. God's concern for the world is shown when his children give. The process is clear—because God gives, his people give, and by these gifts the disenfranchised receive care.

God's economy runs on generosity.

The natural conduit is blocked, however, if God's people fail to give generously. God's economy runs on generosity. God gives his people far more than they need in order that they might give of their abundance to others. In this way, God meets the needs of countless people around his world.

One of the earliest pictures we are given of the New Testament church demonstrates that this spirit of generosity was pervasive. Luke recorded the following:

> And they devoted themselves to the apostles' teaching and the fellowship, to the breaking of bread and the prayers. And awe came upon every soul, and many wonders and signs were being done through the apostles. And all who believed were together and had all things in common. And they were selling their possessions and belongings and distributing the proceeds to all, as any had need. And day by day, attending the temple together and breaking bread in their homes, they received their food with glad and generous hearts, praising God and having favor with all the people. And the Lord added to their number day by day those who were being saved (Acts 2:42–47).

God's people, filled with his Spirit, gathered for biblical teaching and community, and they saw God do astounding works. The church acted like a family. They cared for one another and gave of their possessions to anyone who had need. Like Israel, the way God cared for the needs of others was through the generosity of his people.

Moses ended this section by using a fascinating phrase to describe God's people. He said that they are God's "treasured possession (v. 18)." This is not the first time Moses used that language to speak of God's people (see Deut 7:6). This descriptive phrase referred to a certain portion of a king's royal treasury. While a king would have many possessions, a particular portion of his treasury was unique and special. This "treasured possession" might include prized tokens of battles won, memorials of significant events, or gifts given by other leaders. They were set apart, distinct, and valued above all the rest. You might imagine your "treasured possession" by considering the first items you would want to save if your house caught fire or the last belongings you'd want stolen if a robber plundered your home. These would be your treasured possessions.

God refers to his people as his treasured possession. Yes, God described his people, who were so prone to the sin of idolatry, with this amazing phrase. Despite their constant failings, God continued to pour out his chesed, his loving-kindness, upon them. These people were the treasured possession of the King of Kings.

What does God do with his treasured possession? He placed them in "praise and in fame and in honor high above all the nations that he [had] made (v. 19)." He placed his distinct, holy people in full view of the watching world. There they would testify to his greatness, power, and glory. In a very real way, God gives away his treasured possession—his people—so that they can proclaim his glory to the world.

So, God gives himself to his people, they give back to God as an act of worship and thanks, and then God gives both they and their resources to the world in mission. When God's people give, the needs of people are met, the gospel is proclaimed, God's character is modeled, and the glory of God is seen by a watching world.

Giving is a statement of faith in God. As we give, we are saying that we trust God to provide for our needs in the future. This statement is only made, however, when we give of the first fruits of our possessions to God. If we wait until we've spent everything we need for ourselves to give, then we are not forced to trust God. But, when we give off the top, before we know what else might come, we are saying that we trust the faithful hand of God to meet our needs in the future. Do you trust God in this way? Does your giving to your local church and to the needs of others demonstrate a deep faith in God?

Any discussion of giving is both easy and hard to put into action. It is easy because the application is clear. God gives, so his people give. We give *Faith in Action* generously because God has given generously to us. We then purpose in our hearts and minds to give and do so as an act of worship (2 Cor 9:7). But it is hard to discuss giving because giving requires sacrifice. It means we may not live like our neighbors. We may not have the nicest house, the best car, or enjoy some of the luxuries life offers. This sacrifice seems overwhelming and painful to most. The only power to compel true generous giving is a deep understanding of the gospel. When we consider the giving of God and the price paid by Jesus, we recognize that our giving pales in comparison. The good news of Jesus and the power of the Holy Spirit are capable of producing generosity in your life, and in your church, today.

Prayer Consider your current level of giving and ask God, by his Spirit, to bring conviction and change where needed. Reflect on the profound sacrifice of the cross of Jesus, and allow that to overflow in prayers of praise and consideration of the generosity of your heart. Remember that generous hands demonstrate humility and thankfulness.

Before Your Eyes

Deuteronomy 27:1–8

*And when you have crossed over the Jordan, you shall
set up these stones, concerning which I command you
today, on Mount Ebal, and you shall plaster them with
plaster. And there you shall build an altar to the LORD
your God, an altar of stones. You shall wield no iron tool
on them.*
Deuteronomy 27:4–5

Sight is a precious gift. With it a groom can gaze
at the beauty of his bride as she walks down the wedding
aisle or a mother can marvel at her newborn baby as she
holds him in her arms. Vision allows us to survey the vast
ocean and stare in awestruck wonder at the grandeur of
a magnificent mountain range. Our sight serves a protec-
tive function as well by allowing us to avoid situations that
might cause us harm. Vision allows us to recognize and
avoid the speeding car swerving into our lane or the tod-
dler wandering into the road.

In chapter 27, Moses begins a lengthy conclusion to
the book of Deuteronomy with an object lesson for the nation of Israel. He wanted them to see with their eyes the instructions they had heard with their ears. This show-and-
tell combination provided ample reminders for the people
as they entered the Promised Land.

In many ways, the end of his instructions to the nation parallels what he said at the outset of the book—God

> *Jesus was the only one who chose the narrow way.*

was giving them the land as a gift, and he would continually show himself faithful to his people. Between these bookends, Moses provided clear ethical instruction for the Israelites. Those actions were motivated and powered by the good news message Moses proclaimed at the beginning and end of the book.

Moses instructed the people to set up an altar of large stones on the mountain. The Israelites were to cover the stones with plaster and write the words of the law on the rocks. These words were to be written "very plainly" so that all could see (v. 27:8). The Israelites would not be able to excuse their disobedience because of a lack of knowledge. They had not only heard the law at some time in the past, but also they saw it every day on the mountains overlooking the Promised Land.

Then the nation was to divide into two groups: six of the tribes standing on Mount Gerizim and the other six standing on Mount Ebal. The priestly tribe of Levi would then declare a series of curses that would accompany the disobedience of the nation (27:15–26; 28:15–68) and blessings that would accompany their obedience (28:1–14). These two groups of people would visually symbolize the choice that lie before all people; some would follow the path of blessing and life, while others would follow the path of cursing and death. Jesus used similar imagery at the conclusion of the Sermon on the Mount. He invited his listeners to "enter by the narrow gate (Mt 7:13)." This gate is narrow and its path is difficult, but in the end it leads to life. The other gate is wide and its path is easy, but in the end it results in

> *Faith in Jesus empowers believers to renounce the well word way of death and choose the path that leads to life.*

destruction. Many people walk the wide path; few choose the narrow one (Mt 7:13–14).

In fact, Jesus was the only one who chose the narrow way. He lived in a fallen world yet perfectly fulfilled the law of God. Faith in Jesus empowers believers to renounce the well word way of death and choose the path that leads to life. Sadly, however, many will reject the gracious gift of God and follow the path to their own destruction. These two alternatives were seared into the minds of God's people as they entered the land. The object lessons and visual reminders were meant to call their attention back to God's truth whenever they were forgetful (which was often).

God holds out the same choice for people today. Like Israel, we need constant reminders of the truth of God's Word to reject the voices in our world that clamor for our attention. Everywhere we go, we face a dizzying array of messages designed to capture our attention and compel our actions. Click-bait headlines arrest our incessant scrolling on social media and lure us into their fictitious, and often laughable, tales. With a click, we can learn the dating history of our favorite celebrity, the radical weight loss supplement that actually works (supposedly), life hacks to overcome life's daily frustrations, and the top 10 ways to accomplish pretty much anything you want—all from the comfort of your couch.

Life-shaping messages extend beyond social media, though. Our friends, family, coworkers, and neighbors speak into our lives on a regular basis. Their words shape our decisions, affirm or challenge our thoughts, and determine much about the trajectory of our lives. Parents often discuss the negative effects of peer pressure on their teenage children, yet as long as we live, our peers will influence us. At times, these voices may be helpful—like when your friend from church challenges you in an area of sin and reminds you of the hope of the

> *Without constant vigilance, the message of the gospel can be lost, because what is "out of sight" is often "out of mind."*

> *Through the Word, we can see the example of Jesus, and by the power of his Spirit, follow in his path.*

gospel. More often than not, these voices hijack our minds and cause fear, anxiety, anger, doubt, or bitterness. They can cause us to forget about God, his good purposes for our lives, and the necessity of worshipful obedience in light of his grace. Without constant vigilance, the message of the gospel can be lost, because what is "out of sight" is often "out of mind."

God's people must respond by keeping God and his Word before their eyes and minds on a regular basis. They must plaster his Word on the mountains of their heart so that they might remember and obey. This begins by reading and meditating on God's Word each day. His Word reminds us of his character and His work on our behalf (Lk 24:27). It also illuminates the path to life and shows God's people how to walk on it (Ps 119). Certainly, the Bible will not directly answer every question you face. It will not tell you whom to marry (though it will tell you what kind of person to choose). It will not tell you what job to pursue (though it will tell you how to honor God with your work). And it will not describe God's reasoning behind every form of evil and suffering you face (though it will tell you what he plans to do with evil in the end). God's Word will show you the plan of God to rescue fallen sinners through the substitutionary death and victorious resurrection of Jesus Christ. It will exalt Jesus as the perfect Son of God, who not only died the death his people deserved but also lived the life they were meant to live. Through the Word, we can see the example of Jesus, and by the power of his Spirit, follow in his path. Our Bibles are meant to have the same visual effect that the plaster rocks on the mountains had for the people of God. As we look at the Bible, we see God's son Jesus and are transformed into his image.

Food for
Thought The ideas and images that you most often place before your eyes will fill your mind and influence your heart. Like it or not, you cannot escape the influence of the sights you see on a daily basis. What do you look at most? What influence do these images have? How do they point you toward Christ or away from him?

Faith in
Action

It is not likely that you will be able to plaster any mountains with the law of God, but you can find other ways to keep the Word of God before you. Write a few key Bible passages on a notecard and hang them up in a place you will see every day, such as your bathroom mirror, the refrigerator, or the dash of your car. Passages such as Ephesians 2:1–10 or Romans 5:6–11 would be a great place to begin.

Prayer

God for giving you his Word to remind you of His character and His purposes for your life. Ask him to use his Word to shape your life as you seek to place it before your eyes regularly.

Overconfidence

Deuteronomy 29:18–19

*Beware lest there be among you a man or woman or
clan or tribe whose heart is turning away today from
the LORD our God to go and serve the gods of those
nations. Beware lest there be among you a root bearing
poisonous and bitter fruit, one who, when he hears
the words of this sworn covenant, blesses himself in
his heart, saying, 'I shall be safe, though I walk in the
stubbornness of my heart.' This will lead to the sweeping
away of moist and dry alike.*
Deuteronomy 29:18–19

Overconfidence kills. Every year, a football player
makes the "not-Top 10" list because of it. The lightning
fast tailback breaks through the defensive line, jukes a
linebacker, and outruns the secondary on the way to the
end zone. Ten yards from the score, the deafening sounds
of the exuberant crowd rise to meet him. Then it happens.
He looks up and catches a glimpse of himself in the jum-
botron, and in a moment, he recalls how awesome he is.
Wanting to savor the moment, he slows down and glances
over his shoulder to give a beauty queen-like wave to the
cornerback he left in the dust. Wanting to get a head start
on the touchdown dance he's been practicing since training camp, he drops the ball before crossing the goal line.
The crowd erupts at the stunning display of talent, only

to be silenced by clear evidence of the even more stunning display of ignorance.

Overconfidence kills.

"Pride goes before destruction," says the writer of Proverbs 16:18. Life attests to this reality. While we may appear to have it all figured out, given enough time we will all prove our folly. Sometimes we will do so in comical ways; at other times, we will do so tragically.

Moses already warned the nation against pride as they entered the Promised Land (Deut 8:11–20). Now, it was time to zero in on select individuals within the nation who would rebel against the Lord and pursue the idolatry of the nations. He equated these individuals to a root bearing poisonous or bitter fruit (v. 18). To the outside observer, such people appeared healthy, but they would destroy not only themselves but also those who consumed their evil.

Like the rest of the nation, those individuals heard the covenant promises that God had given his people. Still, they disregarded those promises. What was worse, they didn't feel the least bit of remorse. In fact, they thought they were getting away with their disobedience. Such a person blessed "himself in his heart (v. 19)" rather than seeking the blessing from God. He said, "I shall be safe, though I walk in the stubbornness of my heart (v. 19)." He mistook the gifts God had given the nation with divine acceptance of his sinfulness, assuming that God either didn't see or didn't care about his behavior. Through Moses, God warned that such overconfidence would cause destruction; God would act to judge all wickedness. Moses had previously cautioned the people with the truth that they must

While we may appear to have it all figured out, given enough time we will all prove our folly.

pay the price for their pride and
sin individually (Deut 24:16).

God cautioned the nation
that poisonous and bitter fruit like
this would have implications for
the nation as well (Deut 29:19).
The football player who drops the
ball before he crosses the goal line
costs his entire team six points. In
the same way, the prideful posturing of certain Israelites
would contaminate the nation and lead to the exile.

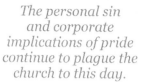

*The personal sin
and corporate
implications of pride
continue to plague the
church to this day.*

The personal sin and corporate implications of
pride continue to plague the church to this day. The humility of God's people within the church is a mark of his kindness at work in his people. The church should be filled with
those who quickly acknowledge and repent of their pride,
seeking to humble themselves before God (James 4:10).
For this to happen, God's people must renounce overconfidence and recognize the ways they continually rationalize
their sin and presume upon the continued favor of God.
For example, a greedy family that fails to give generously
may falsely assume that God will continue to provide for
their luxurious lifestyle. Or, a rebellious teenager may assume that because her parents have not busted her for her
antics that she will get away with them forever. According
to God, this presumption will most assuredly be judged.
Therefore, people who recognize their pride should humble themselves before God is forced to do so.

*The church should be
filled with those who
quickly acknowledge
and repent of their
pride, seeking to
humble themselves
before God.*

Also, God's church must graciously and intentionally speak
truth to those harming the body
through overt disregard for God's
Word. Pride is an individual sin
with corporate implications, so
the church brings harm upon itself when it allows its members
to walk unchecked in their pride.
Paul used this logic to instruct the

church on how it should respond to sexual immorality in the family of God (1 Cor 5). Rather than addressing sin, the church was tolerating heinous evil among its members; the kind that was not even tolerated in pagan nations (1 Cor 5:1).

Paul reminded the Corinthians that by failing to address this sin they were complicit in these evil actions. Like a little leaven, this man's evil was spreading through the whole loaf. Therefore, Paul applied Moses' instructions from Deuteronomy and commanded the church to "purge the evil person from among you (1 Cor 5:13)." In fact, he told them to "deliver this man to Satan for the destruction of his flesh (1 Cor 5:5)." These are countercultural words for the modern church, where sin and evil are often swept under the rug, and everyone pretends like they do not exist. In an effort to show love to others by refusing to judge their actions, we may actually respond in the most unloving way possible—allowing them to remain in their sin and run toward their own destruction. The most loving way we can treat our brothers and sisters in Christ (and the church as a whole) is to privately, clearly, and lovingly address the poisonous root and bitter fruit of pride, and the overconfidence it breeds, before it is too late.

Why are people in the church so reluctant to address sin in one another's lives? What causes you to shrink back from speaking truth to those you love? How can fear hinder this process? Why does it seem that people are so reluctant to receive loving admonition?

You likely recognize blind spots in the lives **Faith in** of others, where they are incapable of seeing **Action** their sin clearly. Sins such as pride, gossip, bitterness, anger, or unbelief are hard to see in isolation. We need our brothers and sisters to help us see our sin, particularly our pride. Take the initiative and seek out someone you trust and ask them a simple question like, "Is there anything you observe in my life that is unfit for one of God's children?" As you do, prayerfully seek out opportunities to humbly do the same for someone you love.

Prayer

Thank God for loving you enough to point out your sin and continually grant you space for humble repentance. Pray that God would show you your pride (in big and small ways) and that he would give you grace to humble yourself rather than continue to presume upon his kindness.

Godly Sorrow

Deuteronomy 30:1–10

*And when all these things come upon you, the blessing
and the curse, which I have set before you, and you call
them to mind among all the nations where the LORD
your God has driven you, and return to the LORD your
God, you and your children, and obey his voice in all
that I command you today, with all your heart and with
all your soul, then the LORD your God will restore your
fortunes and have mercy on you, and he will gather you
again from all the peoples where the LORD your God
has scattered you.*
Deuteronomy 30:1–3

All people sin, but all people do not respond the
same way when they sin. You might remember the first
time your parents caught you doing something that was
clearly against the rules. It may have been hitting your
brother, talking back to your mother, or blatantly lying
about whether or not you ate that last cookie. In that moment, you were confronted with a choice. You could admit your sin, ask for forgiveness and accept your punishment—or not. You could choose to break down in tears,
justify your actions, or compound an already bad situation
with another lie. Far too often, we all chose the wrong op-
tion.

Life will present you with a steady stream of opportunities to respond to your sin, because you will sin often.

> *Life will present you with a steady stream of opportunities to respond to your sin, because you will sin often.*

You will never fully overcome sin in this life, so it is important to learn how to deal with it. In fact, an important mark of maturity in the Christian life is the way in which we recognize and respond to sin.

Moses knew the sinful nature of the nation of Israel, and he concluded the book of Deuteronomy with instructions for how the people should respond to their sins—both at that time, during the Promised Land years, and in the future when they would be sent into exile as a result of their ongoing sins. They simply had to "return to the Lord (v. 2)." Jesus vividly illustrated this principle in his famous story about a prodigal son and his loving father. The son, who squandered his inheritance in wayward living, "came to his senses" and decided to return and beg the father to take him back as a slave (Lk 15:17–19). Jesus described the reunion this way: "And he arose and came to his father. But while he was still a long way off, his father saw him and felt compassion, and ran and embraced him and kissed him (v. 20)." The father took him back, not as a slave, but as his beloved son.

God responds to human sin in the same way. He promised the nation of Israel that he would "restore [their] fortunes and have mercy on [them] (v. 3)." He promises Christians that they will find such mercy too. The author of Hebrews wrote, "Let us then with confidence draw near to the throne of grace, that we may receive mercy and find grace to help in time of need (4:16)."

> *An important mark of maturity in the Christian life is the way in which we recognize and respond to sin.*

Drawing near to God occurs as people repent of their sin. Repentance is a word that describes the process of turning from sin to God. This was Jesus' one-word sermon at the outset of his earthly ministry (Mk 1:15; Mt 4:17). The people needed to repent because the kingdom of God had come in the person of Jesus. Repentance precedes salvation, but it doesn't stop there. Believers must continue the practice of repentance throughout their lives.

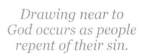

Drawing near to God occurs as people repent of their sin.

Repentance is a definitive mark of a true Christian. Only God's children can repent. Certainly, all people can feel sorry for their actions, embarrassed because they got caught, or shameful for the pain they've caused others. However, these feelings are not genuine repentance. Paul, in his letter to the church in Corinth, contrasted genuine repentance and what he called "worldly grief (2 Cor 7:10)." He commended the Corinthian church for their display of repentance in light of his challenging first letter. He wrote, "For see what earnestness this godly grief has produced in you, but also what earnestness to clear yourselves, what indignation, what fear, what longing, what zeal, what punishment (2 Cor 7:11)!" True repentance is holistic, meaning that every facet of a person's life—his or her actions, emotions, and thoughts—turns from sin and pursues holiness.

Let's consider the all-too-common sin of anger. Imagine that a father comes home from a long day at work only to encounter his four children in rare form. Their continual disobedience, coupled with his not-so-pleasant mood, is a toxic combination. He explodes in a fury, speaks harshly to his children, and disciplines them out of anger rather than love.

True repentance is holistic, meaning that every facet of a person's life—his or her actions, emotions, and thoughts—turns from sin and pursues holiness.

Later, when sitting in his recliner, this father could feel guilt over his anger. He could hang his head in shame when his wife confronts him for crossing the line. Perhaps he might rationalize his actions—blaming his annoying boss for harsh work conditions and his wife for the immaturity of the children. Sorrow may be his companion as he slumps off to bed, but he believes this feeling will go away in the morning. The thought of confessing his sin to God never crosses his mind.

Contrast that scenario with a father who demonstrates genuine repentance. Upon sinning against his children, this man would sense the displeasure of God and have a clear awareness of his disobedience. He would first acknowledge his sin before God and seek the mercy and forgiveness offered to him in Christ (see David's prayer in Psalm 51 after his sin with Bathsheba). Then, the broken father would seek restoration with his children. His feelings of conviction would spill over into his actions, and he would seek out his kids and ask for their forgiveness as well. Then his longing and zeal to honor God would lead to obvious changes in his lifestyle.

The message God gave the nation of Israel at the conclusion of the book of Deuteronomy is also a message of hope for you and me today. No matter what we do, how bad we fail, or how far we run from God, he is willing to receive us back. Yes, the sin of the nation of Israel would lead to their exile from the land of promise, but this would not be the end of their story. God would restore them to the land as an act of amazing grace. And our sin is not the end of our stories, either. God longs to take our sin away—to cast it as far as the east is from the west—because he longs to have fellowship with his children (Ps 103:12). Such inexplicable kindness is meant to lead us to genuine repentance (Rom 2:4).

Food for Thought When is the last time you genuinely repented from sin? God desires for you to grow in repentance throughout your life, and you should find that the longer you walk with Jesus the more you desire to repent quickly and often. Have you learned the pain of broken fellowship with God and the joy of his grace?

Faith in Action

Keep a repentance log. Throughout the day, take note of the times God makes you aware of your sin. Seek to actively repent of that sin and record the steps you are taking to make your sin right with God and anyone else you've wronged. Allow this journal to remind you of the great joy of repentance.

Prayer

Thank God that he is a loving father who allows sinners to repent. Praise his kindness in giving you time to repent and his Spirit who brings your sin to mind. Ask him to grant you the grace to mature in repentance in the coming days.

The Greatness of His Name

Deuteronomy 32:1–4

The Rock, his work is perfect, for all his ways are justice. A God of faithfulness and without iniquity, just and upright is he.
Deuteronomy 32:4

They call it "going out in style." It doesn't take much effort to remember the last famous celebrity, politician, or athlete who ended their career with a bang. This may be with an awe-inspiring play, a memorable speech, or a once-in-a-lifetime movie role. Most of us want to ride into the sunset with everyone thinking about how great we were. We hope go down in the history books as an all-time great.

Moses had that same opportunity as the book of Deuteronomy ended. The life of one of the greatest figures of the Bible was drawing to a close. Soon Moses would die on the top of a mountain outside the Promised Land. These final moments provided him with a chance to celebrate his greatness before the nation. He was, after all, the one who led them from slavery to freedom, and the one who, in spite of the people's incessant complaining, had positioned them to take the Promised Land soon after his death. If anybody had the right to do a little showboating, it was Moses.

> *It is God who has been the hero of the book of Deuteronomy.*

The knowledge of his coming death likely dampened his pride. He knew that he was complicit in the sin of the people. He, too, had been guilty of disregarding God's Word and choosing his own way (Num 20:11–12). His death would confirm that he was a sinner just like everyone else.

Moses knew better than to focus the attention on himself. His climatic final words in the book shift the focus away from himself and towards God. Instead of making much of his own status, Moses resolved, "I will proclaim the name of the Lord (v. 3)." It is God who has been the hero of the book of Deuteronomy, and Moses knew full well that God was the one who had delivered the people, given them his law, led them through the wilderness, broken them of their pride, given them his presence, and brought them to the Promised Land.

Since God is the hero, Moses ended his ministry with a song about the greatness of the Lord. This was not a melody that he hummed alone in his tent, but it was an ascendant chorale that he preached and sang—all while inviting the nation to join in chorus with him. He exhorted his listeners to "ascribe greatness to our God (v. 3)." They should do so because God is a rock—his works are perfect and his ways are just (v. 4). He is faithful, holy, just, and upright.

Each of these characteristics is encapsulated in the concept of "the name of the Lord." The biblical authors used the concept of God's name to refer to the sum total of his attributes. The name of God was to be praised because he alone was perfect. When his name was mentioned, it spoke not of some nebulous deity, but of the God of Abraham, Isaac, and

> *The name of God was to be praised because he alone was perfect.*

Jacob—the one, true, and living God who acted in history to redeem a people to be his (1 Pet 2:9).

We've all probably noticed the influence a name can have upon us. You probably still remember the name of the snarly middle-school teacher who seemed to always have it out for you. Or, you may know the name of your arch-nemesis in high school or the guy or girl who broke your heart. There's no chance that you would name your first child after any of these people. Just hearing their name conjures up memories that you'd like to forget. Their name represents their character.

God's name is meant to have the same effect on his people. God gave Moses his name, "Yahweh," which was meant to define the God who was, is, and will always be (Ex 3:13). As God continued to show himself faithful to his people, they would have increasing reasons to affirm the greatness of his name. Over time, the name of God would induce joy and worship in the hearts of those who knew him as their Savior.

For this reason, prophets like Isaiah said that God's name was the desire of their hearts (Is 26:8). The Psalmist also called people to praise the name of the Lord (Ps 150). Like Moses, all those who have experienced God personally have much to celebrate about the name of the Lord. Our lives, our salvation, and all the good gifts we experience in this life prompt us to praise the name of the Lord. We experience his faithfulness, grace, mercy, love, kindness, discipline, compassion, and care. God's characteristics make his name the desire of our hearts. When we think about him, we should praise his name.

For us to praise God's name, we must change our thinking in

two ways. First, we must think about God often. We should ruthlessly eliminate the distractions and busyness that crowd out an intense focus on God. This kind of focus demands that we seek out times of silence and solitude each day to think about the nature and character of God.

Second, we must think about God rightly. It does no good to think about God if your thoughts do not reflect who God is. For this reason, we must seek to know him through his Word, so that we may conform our thoughts to his revealed character rather than allowing our minds to draw up whatever notions of God our hearts desire. The thoughts we have about God will shape the trajectory of our lives more than anything else.

Food for Thought Often people are influenced by false assumptions about God. For example, when most people hear God described as a Father, they call to mind images of their earthly father. For some, this is a beautiful thought; for others, it is quite painful. We must do the hard work of informing the images of God with biblical content and not merely forming them from personal experience. In order to reshape your view of God, you must dwell on the way in which the Bible speaks of God as a Father and allow those thoughts to transform the ideas you call to mind. Even the best earthly fathers will pale in comparison to the greatness of the Heavenly Father. What false assumptions do you have about God based on your past experiences?

Faith in Action

Make a conscious effort to declare the glory of God's name to those you encounter. This does not mean you have to force an awkward spiritual conversation with everyone you meet. Rather, see if there are ways you can speak about God, his character, and his work in your life in the natural flow of conversations. You will be surprised how many God-given opportunities exist in a given day if you make declaring the awesomeness of God a priority.

Prayer

Spend time today praising the name of the Lord. Call to mind the attributes of God that you are most aware of in your life at this time. Then, take time to consider the attributes of God that are mentioned throughout the Bible. For example, while you may not have a sense of his mercy at this time, be reminded that he is a merciful God at all times—even when you don't recognize it. Meditate on the glorious name of God throughout the day.

The Grip of Grace

Deuteronomy 33:1–5

Yes, he loved his people, all his holy ones were in his hand; so they followed in your steps, receiving direction from you.
Deuteronomy 33:3

If you're like me, life seems out of control most of the time. I used to believe the lie that there would be regular and predicable patterns throughout the course of the year, and if I could just get myself organized, I could find a normal rhythm in which I would thrive. A wife, four kids, a full time job, and a few degrees later, and I now realize the folly of that notion. My schedule is chaotic the moment my feet hit the floor in the morning; such is the nature of life.

But, God does not view life in the same way. The sovereign ruler of all things is never chaotic; he is never overwhelmed by the complexity of life. In fact, the entire Bible testifies to the reality that God is always perfectly executing his good plans and purposes, even in the wake of the destruction caused by human sin. His plans cannot be thwarted, and his purposes will prevail. This is the message of the book of Deuteronomy as well. God's grace will sustain his nation to the end.

Moses was clear that he and the nation as a whole were unworthy of the grace of God. They had continual-

> *The sovereign ruler of all things is never chaotic; he is never overwhelmed by the complexity of life.*

ly been obstinate and unfaithful to the Lord (Deut 32:15–18). For this reason, they had incurred his judgment (32:23–25). Still, God "loved his people" and kept his holy ones in his hands (v. 3). Their inheritance of the land was not based upon their virtue but upon the all-encompassing faithfulness of God. He would not let them go of them. His subsequent blessings on each of the tribes of Israel proved that he cared for every part of the nation (vv. 6–29). God had seen to it that Moses successor, Joshua, would lead the people into the land and fulfill God's long-awaited promise to his people (31:1–8; 34:9–12). Their confidence, however, was not to be rooted in Joshua's ability, but in God who "will not leave you or forsake you (Deut 31:6)." His love will prevail in the end.

Parents recognize an aspect of this type of love because of their relationship with their children. Yes, there are times when they will discipline their precious sons or daughters—at times even allowing their children to experience the consequences of their foolish choices. But, godly parents will never cast their children away. Even if their children are making horrific decisions, they will never cease to belong to their parents.

In a much greater way, God calls his children to himself. He causes them to be born again by the power of his Holy Spirit and saves them (Jn 3). Those he saves—those who receive him and believe in his name—are given the right to be children of God (Jn 1:12). This is an irrevocable status that nothing can change.

Jesus equated his care for his children to that which a shepherd demonstrates for his sheep. He said, "My sheep hear my voice, and I know them, and they follow me. I give them eternal life, and they will never perish, and no one will snatch them out of my hand (Jn 10:27–28)." Jesus then supplied the reason why they were secure: "My Father, who has given them to me, is greater than all, and no one is able to snatch them out of the Father's hand (Jn 10:29)." Jesus used the same language as Moses, noting that God's children are in his hands. Then Jesus said that the hands of God are strong and secure. No one could wrestle them out of the rock-solid grip of the mighty God. Like an infant trying to open his father's clinched fist, nothing and no one can snatch away those whom God is holding.

It's not so much that God's people are holding on to God but that God is holding on to his people.

Notice that the emphasis is on the mighty strength of God to secure his people forever. It's not so much that God's people are holding on to God but that God is holding on to his people. Often our confidence is sabotaged, because we assume that our standing before God rests on how good we've been on any given day. We picture ourselves like a man or woman dangling off of a massive cliff, our only hope of survival dependent upon how tightly we can cling to the rock ledge. We fear that we will surely die if our grip loosens or we grow weary.

Praise God that this is not the picture of the Christian faith presented in his Word! Though it may feel like we are falling, we are always secure in the hand of God. He has us safely harnessed into his care and will not allow anything—even Satan himself—to remove us from his grip! We are secure because God is strong and faithful.

God's faithfulness provides rock-solid confidence for his people. As a result, we can live in victory knowing that we can never sin more than God can forgive. As a result, we need not live in shame, despondency, or despair. God will be faithful to finish the good work he has started (Phil 1:6), and he will see to it that we are one day perfectly conformed

Though it may feel like we are falling, we are always secure in the hand of God.

> *God's faithfulness provides rock-solid confidence for his people.*

to the image of Christ (Rom 8:30). We can also risk our lives, knowing that the worst that can happen to us in this life is death. Remember, "To live is Christ, and to die is gain (Phil 1:21)." We can take the message of the gospel to the dangerous places on the globe knowing that God goes with us. We can be sacrificially generous knowing that God will provide for us. We can face persecution knowing that God will not leave us. When we live with a risky, dangerous faith, we can "do all things through him who strengthens" us (Phil 4:13).

The abrupt conclusion of the book of Deuteronomy demonstrates that the story of the nation would go on. Though Moses' death ended a significant season in their national history, God would continue to lead his people. His care for his people would find its ultimate fulfillment in the arrival of his son Jesus Christ to demonstrate the breadth, length, height, and depth of the love of God, which "surpasses knowledge (Eph 3:19)." From that moment to this, God has continued the work of gathering his people to himself, and we will rule and reign with him over the new heavens and new earth that he will one day establish (Rev 21). We can trust that God will faithfully fulfill all that he has promised to all those who are his. His faithfulness is the theme of Deuteronomy and will be the theme of all eternity. God will accomplish everything he set out to do. We can rest!

Food for Thought

      God's faithfulness is the foundation for human existence. Without it, everything falls apart, but, with it, everything changes. What would change about your life if you lived each day with overwhelming confidence in the faithfulness of God?

Faith in Action

Don't stop here. Let the brilliance of the book of Deuteronomy be a catalyst for picking up another book to study. Consider one of the other titles in this 30 Days series as a prime place to begin. Seek to saturate your life with the life-transforming power of God's Word. Before you close this study, though, take a minute and list your top-ten observations from the book of Deuteronomy. Along with each observation, note a corresponding point of application to guide you in obeying what God has shown you.

Prayer

Thank God for his faithfulness to you. Praise him for allowing you to finish a study through the book of Deuteronomy and for his great grace in preserving this book as a living treasure for his church. Pray that God would overwhelm you with his faithfulness and grace and that you would worship him well in response.

Finding L.I.F.E. in Jesus!

Everyone wants to be happy. The hard part is determining exactly what that means. For some, happiness is defined through relationships. They believe that popularity, a huge friend list on Facebook, and a significant other produces happiness. For others, happiness is defined through success. They believe that personal achievement, a huge number in their bank account, and plenty of expensive toys produces happiness. For still others, happiness is defined through community. They believe that personal growth, a huge impact for societal change, and embracing diversity produces happiness. And these things do—until they don't.

Experiencing happiness is as difficult as catching the greased pig at the county fair. It appears to be right in front of us, but then it slips through our fingers and is gone. Friends, achievement, and personal growth have the potential to bring happiness into our lives, but when our friends disappear, success eludes us, and we realize that we're incapable of self–transformation, happiness is quickly replaced by disillusionment and depression. The problem with pursuing happiness is that it is an emotion that is driven by our circumstances. And let's be honest— we all tend to have more negative than positive experiences in our lives.

So, what's the answer? Should we keep doing the same things while expecting different results, or should we consider what Jesus has to say about finding our purpose for life? If you want to stay on the hamster wheel while you try to catch up to happiness, you can stop reading here. But if you're ready to consider what God wants to do in your life, please read on.

God never promises happiness in the Bible. Are you surprised to hear that? Instead, he promises something much greater—joy. While happiness is an emotion fueled by circumstance, joy is an attitude fueled by God's Spirit. Happiness is self–determined. In other words, I am the sole determiner of whether I'm happy at any given moment. Joy, on the other hand, is God–determined. God has promised to give us joy, and it isn't based on our circumstances—it's based on God's character and promises.

This is why Jesus never talks about giving people happiness. He knew all too well that chasing happiness is like chasing your shadow. You can never catch it. Instead, he talks about giving people life. He said, "I came that they may have life and have it abundantly (Jn 10:10)." Here, Jesus reveals that the thing people really want, whether they know it or not, is abundant life. To have an abundant life means that you are personally satisfied in all areas of your life, and you experience peace and contentment as a result. Jesus' statement also means that we do not have the capacity to create that kind of life for ourselves. Jesus came in order to give it to us. But how? The Bible tells us that achieving this kind of satisfied life requires us to know something about God, ourselves, and the reason for the death and resurrection of Jesus Christ.

First, we must understand God's **love**. The Bible says that God is love (I Jn 4:8), and God created us so that we could know him and experience his love (Gen 1:26–31). God created us to be worshipers and to live forever in the reality of his glory. And, when sin marred his perfect creation, he created a plan to free men and women from its curse. At just the right time in history, God sent his own Son, Jesus, into our world. "For God so loved the world, that he gave his only Son, that whoever believes in him should not perish but have eternal life (Jn 3:16)." It is

God's love that motivates him to restore relationship with those who are separated from him by sin.

Second, we must understand our **isolation**. To be isolated is to be separated from someone, and as a result, to be alone. This is what sin has done to us. It has separated us from the very one we were created to know, love, and worship—God. When Adam and Eve rebelled against God by breaking the lone command he had given them, the entire world was brought under the curse of sin (Gen 3). As a result, God removed them from the Garden of Eden, and their perfect fellowship with God was broken. In an instant, they had become isolated from God because of their sin. From that moment to this, every person born into this world is guilty of sin. The Bible says, "For all have sinned and fall short of the glory of God (Rom 3:23)." Because of this "there is none righteous, no, not one (Rom 3:10)." Further, "The wages of sin is death (Rom 6:23a)." We were created to love and worship God in perfect community, but now because of sin we are isolated from him. Meanwhile, we try to satisfy this desire to know God by pursuing our own happiness, even though we can never hope to attain it. And in doing so, we risk being isolated from God for all eternity.

Third, we must understand our need for **forgiveness.** There is only one way to experience God's love and escape the isolation caused by sin—we must experience God's forgiveness. In spite of sin, God never stopped loving the people he created. He promised Adam and Eve that he would send someone who could fix the problem they had created. When it was time, God sent his own Son, Jesus, to be the world's Savior. This, too, was an act of God's love. The Bible says, "God shows his love for us in that while we were still sinners, Christ died for us (Rom 5:8)." When Jesus died on the cross, he was paying the penalty for our sins (Rom 3:23–26). When God raised Jesus from the dead, it was to demonstrate that forgiveness was available to all who would receive it by faith. Paul explained how this happens in his letter to the Ephesians. "For by grace you have been saved through faith. And this is not your own doing; it is the gift of God, not a result of works, so that no one may boast (Eph 2:8–9)."

The reality is that we cannot experience salvation as a result of our own efforts. We can try to be a good person, go to a church, even give a ton of money to worthy causes—none of these "works" can provide forgiveness. No matter how hard we try, we will always "fall short of the glory of God." That is why we must receive God's offer of forgiveness and salvation by faith. Faith simply means to trust or believe. Salvation requires us to believe that God loves us, that we are isolated from him by our sins, and that his Son Jesus died and was raised to life again to pay the sin debt that we owe God because of our sins. When we take God up on his offer of the gift of salvation, he doesn't just give us forgiveness—he gives us life! The Bible says, "The free gift of God is eternal life in Christ Jesus our Lord (Rom 6:23)."

Fourth, we must understand the **enjoyment** that comes from knowing, loving, and worshiping God. Whether we know it or not, we are slaves to sin until God sets us free (Rom 6:20–23). This was the ultimate reason that God sent his Son, Jesus, to die on the cross for our sins—God sent Jesus so that we could be set free from our sins. Jesus said, "You will know the truth, and the truth will set you free. . . . Everyone who commits sin is a slave to sin. . . . So, if the Son sets you free, you will be free indeed (Jn 8:32–36)." Jesus was teaching us that we must be set free from sin in order to enjoy the life that God has given us—both now and in eternity future. We are set free when we commit our lives to Jesus Christ through faith in his death and resurrection. Then, and only then, will we find joy in the abundant life of Jesus Christ!

So, the question for you is a simple one: Are you ready to experience freedom from sin and the abundant life that Jesus promised you? If so, God is waiting for to talk with him about it (Jer 29:13). Stop right where you are and make this your prayer to God,

"Father in heaven, I know that I'm a sinner. I know that I've done lots of things that displease you and disappoint you. And, I know that I'm isolated from you because of my sin. I know that if I die without knowing you, I will spend forever separated from you in hell. But, I believe that Jesus is your sinless Son, and I believe that he died on the cross for me. I believe that he died to provide a perfect payment for my sin debt. I believe that you raised him from the dead so that I could experience forgiveness for my sins. Right now, Father, I'm asking you to forgive me of my sins and save me. I am receiving your Son Jesus as my personal Lord and Savior. I will follow you the rest of my life. Please give me the joy of a life spent knowing, loving, and worshiping you. I ask these things in Jesus' name, Amen."

If you made the decision to accept Jesus as your Savior today, we want to talk with you! Please contact the people at www.seed–publishing–group.com. We would love to talk with you about your decision and help you with your first steps in following Jesus!

If you enjoyed *30 Days to Deuteronomy*, check out the other books in the *30 Days to the Bible* series.

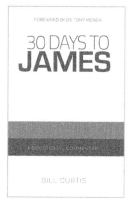

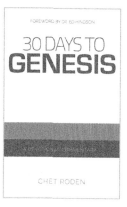

Also from Seed Publishing:

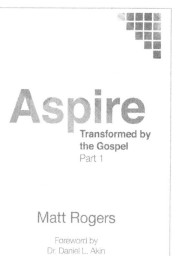
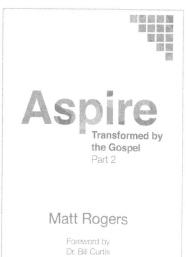

Made in the USA
Middletown, DE
27 January 2023

22549765R00116